Charlie Chaplin's *Modern Times*

This book looks at Charlie Chaplin's masterpiece, *Modern Times* (1936), through the lens of film aesthetics, structure, and post-modern perspective.

The naïve Tramp character of *Modern Times* is often seen as the embodiment of a revolutionary reaction to his age. However, this study of the film shows that it is not only difficult but also impossible to accept the long-established critical reception of Chaplin's film and its characters in our own "*Post-modern Times*." Drawing from extensive research and bringing post-modern context to the film through a comparative analysis of Todd Phillips's *Joker* (2019), the book introduces how exhilarating a comprehensive study of film can be for engaged viewers.

Illustrating that a detailed filmic reading of *Modern Times* can be a guide, or an extended case study, for analysing culture, this book will be of interest to students and teachers in film studies, literary studies, and the visual arts.

Carl Peters is a scholar, curator, and author of *bpNichol Comics* (2002); *textual vishyuns: image and text in the work of bill bissett* (2011); and *Studies in Description*, the first annotated study of the entire text of Gertrude Stein's *Tender Buttons* (2016).

Figure 0.1 Tramp in the crowd

Charlie Chaplin's *Modern Times*
The Work of Life in the Age
of Mechanical Reproducibility

Carl Peters

Routledge
Taylor & Francis Group
LONDON AND NEW YORK

First published 2022
by Routledge
2 Park Square, Milton Park, Abingdon, Oxon OX14 4RN

and by Routledge
605 Third Avenue, New York, NY 10158

Routledge is an imprint of the Taylor & Francis Group, an informa business

© 2022 Carl Peters

The right of Carl Peters to be identified as author of this work has been asserted in accordance with sections 77 and 78 of the Copyright, Designs and Patents Act 1988.

All rights reserved. No part of this book may be reprinted or reproduced or utilised in any form or by any electronic, mechanical, or other means, now known or hereafter invented, including photocopying and recording, or in any information storage or retrieval system, without permission in writing from the publishers.

Trademark notice: Product or corporate names may be trademarks or registered trademarks, and are used only for identification and explanation without intent to infringe.

British Library Cataloguing-in-Publication Data
A catalogue record for this book is available from the British Library

Library of Congress Cataloging-in-Publication Data
Names: Peters, Carl Lynden, 1965- author.
Title: Charlie Chaplin's Modern times : the work of life in the age of mechanical reproducibility/Carl Peters.
Description: Abingdon, Oxon ; New York, NY : Routledge, 2022. | Includes bibliographical references and index.
Identifiers: LCCN 2021035262 (print) | LCCN 2021035263 (ebook) | ISBN 9780367339838 (hardback) | ISBN 9781032180267 (paperback) | ISBN 9780429323317 (ebook)
Subjects: LCSH: Chaplin, Charlie, 1889–1977-Criticism and interpretation. | Little Tramp (Fictitious character) | Modern times (Motion picture) | Work in motion pictures. | Motion pictures-United States-History-20th century.
Classification: LCC PN1997.M639 P48 2022 (print) | LCC PN1997.M639 (ebook) | DDC 791.430973/0904-dc23
LC record available at https://lccn.loc.gov/2021035262
LC ebook record available at https://lccn.loc.gov/2021035263

ISBN: 978-0-367-33983-8 (hbk)
ISBN: 978-1-032-18026-7 (pbk)
ISBN: 978-0-429-32331-7 (ebk)

DOI: 10.4324/9780429323317

Typeset in Times New Roman
by Apex CoVantage, LLC

This book is dedicated to the memory of Jerry Zaslove

Contents

List of figures viii
Acknowledgements ix
Preface: the art of seeing x

1 Work 1

2 Life 34

3 A comedian sees the world 68

   Postscript: meanwhile 100

Works cited 106
Index 110

Figures

0.1	Tramp in the crowd	ii
1.1	The president with his Tarzan comic	7
1.2	The Tramp strapped in the feeding machine	8
1.3	Red flag (long shot)	21
1.4	Red flag (close-up)	21
1.5	Jail cell view of Tramp inside "his comfortable cell" from outside	30
2.1	Dream home	43
2.2	Dream home (when the cop enters the shot)	43
2.3	Roller skating (scene from *Joker*)	51
2.4	Fleck watches Chaplin (scene from *Joker*)	52
2.5	Ellen models her robe/coat	54
2.6	"Bedroom display"	55
2.7	The ramshackle home	57
2.8	Breakfast table with comics	58
2.9	The Tramp as feeding machine	65
3.1	"A pretty girl and a gay old man"	88
3.2	Singing waiter just before he is about to sing	91
3.3	Closing image (Tramp and Ellen on the divided highway) frontal	96
3.4	Image of Tramp and Ellen from behind	97

Acknowledgements

I have always thought that all writing is construction. It takes work lifting the heavy parts. There are no light parts—I want to thank Karl Siegler, Jerry Zaslove, Ken Harmel, Jennifer Vennall, Graham Mears, and my loving wife Kimberly.

Preface
The art of seeing

> The work of art is valuable only in so far as it is vibrated by the reflexes of the future.
>
> (André Breton cited in Walter Benjamin "The Work of Art in the Age of Mechanical Reproducibility")

Time is of the essence. And, as John Berger points out, "*All creation is in the art of seeing.*"[1] Simply put, Charlie Chaplin's 1936 film *Modern Times* can no longer be considered to represent the "modern times" of our age. It appears that its audiences' presumed long-standing love affair with the film's Tramp has tended to dumbfound and overwhelm the vast majority of critical interpretations of the film for almost a century since its making. The assumption these persistent reactions to and interpretations of the character of the Tramp make is that he looks at life through the eyes of a child, a naive observer as he "innocently" bumbles along. But we can only love this comic character if we can manage to avoid objectively seeing what is happening to him in his time. He simply does not seem to know fully, nor understand his world well enough, when he acts; thus, the consequences of his actions seem comic. But if we do not identify with its main character and look at the film in its historical context, then we see the debris and remnants of his actions as disastrous, not as hilarious. The machines of Chaplin's modern times of the mid-1930s dehumanize all the film's characters—the Tramp, his associates, as well as the "gamine." In *Modern Times*, industrialization affects all the characters: from "the factory boss nursing his ulcers," as recorded in Chaplin's preliminary notes, to the unemployed workers in the street (*Chaplin: His Life and Art* 460).[2]

This study of *Modern Times* attempts to show that it is not only difficult but also actually impossible to accept the long-established critical reception of Chaplin's film and its characters in our own "*Post-modern Times*."

A transformation of "traditional" audience perceptions of *Modern Times* to those of almost a century later is accomplished by the 2019 film, *Joker*, which uses Chaplin's 1936 film as its central structural element. The critical reception of *Modern Times* to date has not accounted for its historicity, a historicity clearer to us in retrospect from our vantage point in the 21st century. If there was ever any doubt of Chaplin's film being a classic of its genre, that doubt is put to rest when *Modern Times* appears midway through director Todd Phillips's film *Joker* as its own turning point.

Films, to borrow an expression from the film critic and historian Jay Leyda, "beget" films. *Joker*, for example, "finds, acquires, and seizes"—instructs—the spectator to see Chaplin's film through the critical lens of the "post-modern" present, whereas "modern" critics such as those represented in Richard Schickel's *The Essential Chaplin* tend to view *Modern Times* outside of history. Phillips's film, in fact, deconstructs *Modern Times*, which is, in a word, the methodology of post-modernism. *Joker* makes certain demands on the viewer—it insists that we re-evaluate the film *Modern Times* with scepticism. "I think you'd have to watch *Modern Times*," Phillips comments, "because we believe there is some Chaplin in [Arthur Fleck] that I think is really important."[3] He has also said that Joker's costume is inspired by that of Charlie Chaplin's Tramp. What is that "something of Chaplin" in Phillip's character, Joker, is the question we will seek to answer.

Charlie Chaplin's Tramp is an enigmatic representation of the modern man *in* the modern times of the 1930s. He is swept up and carried along by the "modern" (contemporary) socio-economic currents of his age, in which he remains a vagabond who comically struggles with his fate. As we will see, he places himself (or, more often than not, his circumstances place him) into many roles that include—in addition to a factory worker—shipyard worker, thief, night watchman and waiter, but he seems most comfortable when placed (often of his own volition) as a prisoner living in "his comfortable prison cell." Exactly halfway through the film, his passive acquiescence to his storm-tossed fate will be tested by a woman. And he will continue to fail.

Richard Schickel, in "The Tramp Transformed," comments that there is what can be called an unruly darkness beneath Chaplin: "the Tramp was never himself wretched . . . he pursued bourgeois contentment not revolution" (24). It is this darkness that is taken to the extreme in *Joker*. *Joker*'s character is carefully developed in Phillips' film—his past is explicated to us as a mystery: either he is the "illegitimate" child of the domestic servant Penny Fleck and Thomas Wayne, scion to an enormously wealthy and powerful family; or, in order to avoid an embarrassing scandal, the Wayne family has paid to have official documents created that "prove" he was adopted, then neglected, and abused by Penny and her subsequent lovers as a child. As a result of his inability to solve this binary mystery concerning his origins both of which are negative options, "the Joker" becomes less enigmatic and ever more wilfully psychotic in his actions. The Tramp, however, remains an enigmatic figure throughout—an enduring, almost endearing, and trouble-making, vexing and troublesome presence—who just "shows up"; he is a moving trope in *Modern Times*, the meaning of which is always to be found exclusively within whatever context he occupies. In *Modern Times*, the characters are static and undeveloped—it is the situations, not the characters, which are developed.

While Chaplin's character (the "Tramp") appears happiest in confined spaces, Arthur Fleck (the "Joker") is clearly unhappy and feels out of place in most spaces. A scene from Chaplin's film *Modern Times* actually appears as a central element in Todd Phillips's film, which explores the development and the ultimate metamorphosis of the character "Arthur Fleck." A marketing blurb suffices as a superficial summary: "In Gotham City, mentally troubled comedian Arthur Fleck is disregarded and mistreated by society. He then embarks on a downward spiral of revolution and bloody crime. This path brings him face-to-face with his alter-ego: the Joker."[4] Like most marketing hype, however, this plot summary/description of the film is misleading—we see "Arthur Fleck" in the opening scene of the movie, before any of the actions the marketing blurb alludes to take place, putting on his identity as a clown—his "alter ego"—by painting his face in front of a makeup mirror, at the end of which a tear runs from his eye and begins to dissolve his face paint.

Unlike the Tramp, whom Chaplin explicitly announces with a scene card as "happy in his comfortable cell," Fleck asserts: "I haven't been happy one minute of my entire fucking life." In *Joker*, Fleck learns to deconstruct the fantasy, the falsity, and the construct of assumptions behind the Utopian "story of industry, of individual enterprise—humanity crusading in the pursuit of happiness" of *Modern Times*. And in this he is, in fact, closer to Chaplin the author than he is to that author's creation—the Tramp. He is not as amusing as the Tramp, but rather, as we will see, much more frightening because he is not fooled by a society which otherwise seems inhumanely, mechanically and objectively uncaring. Chaplin, the author, is acutely aware of the dehumanization of others by the modern industrialized society of his day, and the absurdity of its forms of authoritarianism that he can't imagine anyone wanting to be a part of or having a part in. This complete disconnect between Chaplin's tacit complicity with his audience as an author, and his totally inappropriate interactions as a character within his world, is the very basis of the comedy *Modern Times*.

On the other hand, as a depiction of society frozen in a paralysing state of utterly corrupt and ubiquitously pervasive capitalism that diminishes and ridicules all constructive individual aspirations and achievement, as well as cancelling most social services—from psychological counselling of the mentally ill to garbage collection on the city streets—Arthur Fleck's act of shooting three "Wall Street Guys" in a subway (obviously based on the 1984 "subway vigilante" Goetz's shooting of four alleged "criminals") galvanizes an already frustrated, angry, populist mob of looters who adopt his meme as their collective identity and ramp up their anarchic rioting. In a clear reference to the "Occupy Movement" that began on 17 September 2011, on Wall Street in New York City, "the people" in Joker are not "crusading in the pursuit of happiness," but smashing the state that has taken from them every opportunity for happiness other than the one it forces them to put on—the painted (false) smile of an abused clown. But when that smile becomes real, the clown's double appears and that double is no longer amusing—it is frightening and deadly. "Revenge is sweet."

In a *New Yorker* article on Wagner's influence on cinema, Alex Ross comments that when

> Charlie Chaplin watched Leni Riefenstahl's 1935 film *Triumph of the Will*, his immediate impulse, according to Luis Buñuel, was to burst into laughter. The orator on screen seemed to be an insane variation on Chaplin's Little Tramp persona, down to the toothbrush moustache.
> (20)

Looking back at *Modern Times* from the standpoint of the present is a pedagogical exercise. Looking forward from Chaplin's point of view, it becomes chillingly prescient. Embedded in Ross' comment are revelations we have taken for granted, but perhaps deserve a closer look: "For some viewers, Chaplin's idealism may seem wincingly naïve, just as his lampoon of Hitler may seem to trivialize Nazi horrors. Yet naïveté is at the core of Chaplin's enduring appeal" (20).

The "comedy" of *Modern Times*, then, is grounded in its "false belief" in a system that promises happiness, with the caveat that it must be "pursued"—that it can be acquired—and if it is, that the system will reward and provide for you. The audience is made to share that view, and when it does, it does so with more than a touch of irony. The characters in *Modern Times* have internalized the pursuit of happiness their age has encouraged in them at the expense of their humanity, which the system cynically exploits. In *Modern Times*, Chaplin enigmatically stages the illusion of the myth of the modern in its totalitarian forms, from industrialization to fascism, the subject of his next film: *The Great Dictator*.

Joker, with its references to Chaplin's film, unmasks the Tramp portrayed in *Modern Times*, and in this unmasking, a post-modern reading of *Modern Times* is revealed and illuminated. Perhaps the most astonishing accomplishment of Chaplin's film is that it uses the very technologies and techniques of mechanization and standardization of the machine age—the spooling of still images through sets of gears to create the illusion of both movement and time—to create a facsimile of a life lived in the pathos of modernist reality—"a fearful symmetry"[5]—which others such as William Blake described and prophesized in his poetry, and Mary Shelley critiqued in her visionary novel *Frankenstein*. Chaplin is not the first artist to critique "progress"; in this regard, he was not unique, but his approach to the comoedic emphasizes the interrelationship between situations and characters: "The best ideas grow out of the situation," and "you cannot be funny without a funny situation. You can do something clownish, perhaps stumble, but you must have a funny situation"; moreover, "you treat it with a complete reality," he concludes—with *candour* (Meryman 361). Perhaps, Chaplin's most prescient and devastating critique of "progress" and modern times occurs in a department store where the Tramp is hired as a night watchman, and roller skates blindfolded between warning signs of clear and present danger.[6] The self-applied blindfold removes the danger from the Tramp's view but that does not mean it is absent in his situation. He *wilfully* makes himself blind to the danger of his situation (as he does, metaphorically, in every situation throughout the film)—we see it and the gamine responds to and saves him from it. His deliberate blindness consumes him while it entertains and mesmerizes the world; it is shattered by the gamine who saves him from an unfortunate fall. It is this scene from *Modern Times* that appears in *Joker* when Arthur Fleck enters the theatre during a black-tie fundraiser in pursuit of Thomas Wayne, whom he has been led to believe by his mother to be his "real" father.

The Tramp's relationship with the gamine, though based on a shared fantasy, is presented as real to life. On the other hand, Arthur Fleck's relationship with his love interest, Sophia, is presented as purely imaginary. The only "intimate" relationship that Fleck experiences is with his mother. He takes care of her—right up until he euthanizes her. Fleck's mother is a type of double agent—her death announces the birth of his alter ego. Fleck stills his mother's voice by suffocating her; Chaplin, on the other hand, gives his alter ego the Tramp voice when he is instructed to speak by the gamine in the final act in *Modern Times*.

If the "comoedic" as it relates to "comedy" is the presentation of life as it is lived, then this study, *Charlie Chaplin's Modern Times: The Work of Life in the Age of Mechanical Reproducibility*, is a reading of the film as it is experienced in *this* time —"our" time—*post-modern* time. A literal reading of scenes reveals a previously unrecognized critical reality foundational to *Modern Times* from the vantage point of our current historical age that is more than the sum of its parts. This study extends the unmasking of the film classic implied by *Joker*. Peter Schickel asserts that in "their response to *Modern Times*," critics have to date expressed "a sort of indulgent disappointment. People wanted to go on loving Chaplin in the old way," he concludes (27). The film, he comments,

> has some nice stuff—Chaplin and Goddard blithely roller-skating on the edge of the abyss, a funny little piece in which Chaplin is a harassed waiter trying to serve too many customers in a crowded restaurant. But these are sequences that Chaplin might well have concocted fifteen or twenty years earlier. They have nothing to do with the movie's eponymous theme.
>
> (26–27)

They might have nothing to do with the "movie's eponymous theme" if we see them from a nostalgic point of view, but if we consider them from the vantage point of the present, they take on a profoundly prescient meaning. Here, we must be mindful of Chaplin's whole vision: "I was beginning to think of comedy in a structural sense," he writes, "and to become conscious of its architectural form. Each sequence implied the next sequence, all of them relating to the whole" (*My Autobiography* 208). We will explore the construction of crucial images and scenes since Chaplin's "continuity script" for *Modern Times* is no less than a list of the events.[7] And since a film is made of images and scenes, let us see where the art of seeing takes us—let's look at the "nuts and bolts" of *Modern Times* in which "indulgent" gags become prescient situations. Then, the joke will be on the age itself.

The actions of the Tramp in *Modern Times* become assimilated and transformed in the character of Arthur Fleck in the post-modern time of *Joker*. Fleck seems almost smitten by the Tramp when he sees the scene in the department store on screen in the Wayne Theatre, and his quiet laughter seems almost gentle—endearing.[8] Here again, we experience a crucial difference. Chaplin responds to a public, historical and devastating depression; Arthur Fleck is depression internalized—a narcissistic loser. However, it is *Modern Times* which can yet inform our current post-modern anxieties waiting for another catastrophe to happen—Fleck laughs at Chaplin; Chaplin laughs at Riefenstahl.

The Tramp's apparent naïveté is a work of artistic intent which drives and directs the director's critique of socio-economic reality in *Modern Times*.

The fact of Chaplin's "enduring appeal" puts a lie to the expression that his caricature of a mad dictator in *The Great Dictator* "trivializes Nazi horrors." There is poverty and death in *Modern Times* that is no less diminished—"trivialized"—by a so-called "wincingly naïve" Tramp.[9] He endures many storms, only, we will show, to live again in Arthur Fleck's post-*Modern Times* world. The Tramp remains, to cite Sergei Eisenstein's perception of him, "the true and touching 'Holy Innocent,' whose image," for a moment, defines Arthur Fleck's ambition—to *be*, to assume the identity of, to be recognized and validated by his world as, a comedian: a joker critical of his own time—a really funny man.[10]

    Modern Times constructs two figures of the Tramp: life before the gamine—this is the Tramp as a "factory worker" who reverts to the bumbling iconic character audiences have come to know; and life after the gamine—this is the Tramp as a "singing waiter" who proves that he can speak for himself—but only in gibberish. The gamine transforms him, and we will be exploring that transformation more closely in Chapters 2 and 3. And whereas Arthur Fleck chooses his alter ego, his "identity" in the end, Chaplin chooses the Tramp's "other," a real person. He chooses the gamine—he chooses "Ellen."

Notes

1. See https://quotefancy.com/quote/1053004/John-Berger-All-creation-is-in-the-art-of-seeing
2. In the final cut of *Modern Times* we see only the secretary handing the CEO of the "Electro Steel Company" pills and a glass of water.
3. "12 Details and References You May Have Missed in *Joker*." www.insider.com/joker-dc-references-easter-eggs-breakdown-2019-10
4. The Internet Movie Database available @ www.imdb.com/title/tt7286456/
5. William Blake, "The Tyger" in *Songs of Innocence and Experience*.
6. George A. Romero's *Dawn of the Living Dead* (1978) puts zombies on an escalator in a department store mall guided by muzak making a similar statement in a much darker context.
7. BFI | Features | Charlie Chaplin | Chaplin resources available @ http://chaplin.bfi.org.uk/resources/
8. According to Byung-Chul Han, in his work *The Disappearance of Rituals: A Topology of the Present*, "Where resonance disappears completely, depression arises" (10–11). There is no "ritual" in *Modern Times*. Everything becomes overwhelmed by "standardization" in *Modern Times*.
9. Adorno comments that the "workday extends limitlessly in the film" in his essay "Chaplin Times Two." The totality of the culture of the "modern" pervades everything Chaplin touches and drives the character of the Tramp to the brink. He becomes an appendage of the machine and in being driven to the brink he "shows" his failed resistances to the world of "modern times" which is always threatening to make the Tramp obsolete, to extinguish him.

10 Eisenstein is likely referring to age-old Russian motifs that are pervasive in Russian folklore and popular literature and wandering holy figures from Eastern Orthodoxy and I think he is drawing aesthetic "energy" from that context, just as Shklovsky does in how he sees figures in films, who are not allegorically or symbolically presented, but as part of life itself. Chaplin's greatest illusion is the Tramp's innocence & "wincing naïveté." "Happiness" is another matter and seems absent from the start. [Eisenstein's expression of the Tramp as "Holy Innocent" is cited by Alex Ross in "Wagner in Hollywood: A Composer's Fractured Legacy in Film." *The New Yorker*, 31 Aug. 2020, 18–24. (Jerry Zaslove, email message to author 13 Apr. 2021)].

1 Work

The first image in *Modern Times* is of a clock ticking. It touches on the absurd—the experience of watching a recording of time as it passes in a film that is called *Modern Times*, which can only be modern *now*, after the fact, because of its title. The present spectator of *Modern Times* is never contemporary with the time of the film's creation—*Modern Times* is historical time from the point of view of where the spectator is now. In Walter Benjamin's sense, its "modernity" is experienced as "inauthentic."[1] The opening images are almost nostalgic. Their silence is mute—they say: this *was* what it was like; these *were* modern times:

> A factory worker . . .
> . . . CHARLIE CHAPLIN
> A gamin . . .
> . . . PAULETTE GODDARD

And if that isn't clear enough, we have a whole story set down before us which proves, in the end, to be not only a comedy but also something else altogether—a documentary—something to evoke more than laughter; "to add another dimension to my films," Chaplin asserts, "besides that of comedy" (*My Autobiography* 4). Poverty is more than laughter in Chaplin's "modern times"; "This attitude of wanting to make poverty attractive for the other person is annoying. I have yet to know a poor man who has nostalgia for poverty, or who finds freedom in it" (Chaplin in *My Autobiography* 267).

"*Modern Times*. A story of industry, of individual enterprise—humanity crusading in the pursuit of happiness" its title card reads—the alleged human condition of its day. Its "story" will be documented from the standpoint of its two main characters—the Tramp and the "gamine"—and not solely from the Tramp's viewpoint. Indeed, as Chaplin's biographer David Robinson points out, "the scenes of the Gamin's troubles before her meeting the Tramp are among the very rare instances in Chaplin's films . . . where

DOI: 10.4324/9780429323317-1

there is an independent secondary and parallel line of action running alongside the narrative of the Tramp's misadventures" (*Chaplin: His Life and Art* 459). The "gamine's" story, however, is not secondary to the film: her role as a main, rather than incidental character is what adds another dimension to Chaplin's art "besides that of comedy."

The audience is looking at a work of art which depicts the Tramp looking at life. But he's doing so in a work of art. Both experiences—the audience's and the Tramp's—are unsettling; displacing—almost like "Being in the wrong place," as Viktor Shklovsky puts it, "not recognizing things—this is the eternal topic of art" (Shklovsky 358).[2] The film and its story is prospective. The spectator—like the Tramp—never knows what to expect:

> they go inadvertently into a theatre or they look up and see something that they feel, they're in the mood, and they would like to see—and I think—they go in. And it's all by chance. They don't know what they're going to see beforehand.
>
> (*Charlie Chaplin: Interviews* 114)

Times change; in the making of the film, "modern" becomes "historical," then emblematic of its age—"classic." But it is the "times" that are modern, and not the Tramp, since "modern" means "a person who advocates or practices a departure from traditional styles or values." The Tramp of *Modern Times* is emphatically not that; however, it remains to be seen—he does become very briefly "modern" in a very specific way at the end of the film. And even though the title puts the march of time—of which Chaplin is acutely aware—in plain view from the outset (the clock advances from the opening scene), the audience is not ready nor is it prepared for the Tramp's transformation at the end of the film. Shklovsky's point is proven true in Todd Phillips' film, *Joker*, when Arthur Fleck, in the Wayne Theatre, is looking at the "same" work of art—*Modern Times*—in retrospect, laughing with the audiences' laughter—becoming part of it—this wannabe "joker" of post-modern times. In *Modern Times*, more than anything else, it is the recorded salesman of the feeding machine who serves as an agent—a meme—of the displacement and disembodiment of the age.

The film opens with an image of pre-modern times, of agrarian society, of herded sheep. *Modern Times* is no longer the world of the shepherd; *Modern Times* is the world of the Capitalist boss, the age of mechanized, industrialized society, in which human workers rush to the factory like sheep to the shearing pens.

The opening images of the "crusading" masses (the original provisional titles for the film were "The Masses" and/or "The Commonwealth") beg the question of the conditions of the "pursuit of happiness", but these images serve to establish the ethos of the film, and how we are to watch and see "modern times"—that is, in historical context. The opening montage of herded sheep (with one black sheep among them) fading into factory workers exiting a subway, entering a factory and punching timecards is an image that stands out in the opening few moments of the movie, which looks and feels like a documentary or short parody of a propaganda film. It is an image that establishes Chaplin's trope. The Tramp, another black sheep, will ground the brutal truth of the film—sheep, like workers, do what they are told, and black sheep have little or no value or use beyond their bodies—their wool cannot be dyed in any colour other than its own.

So, the Tramp as a worker is already meat for the grinder in *Modern Times*. The metaphor of herded sheep extends to the workers on the assembly line, where we first recognize Chaplin's Tramp in his role as an incompetent factory worker; and the assembly line itself becomes a metaphor for film, since film and assembly lines consist of a series of interchangeable "parts" (scenes, episodes constructed of still images) assembled in a sequence that add up producing a final product—in this case—the "whole" film *Modern Times*. In an extended conceit, every scene in the film is a microcosm of "modern times"; moreover, every gag is a metaphor for its overall narrative—its "message"—and when the audience's attention is made to shift, the gag—the joke—is revealed.

Here, we put our finger on the joke that the opening scene constructs. Chaplin is showing us Henry Ford's America because *Modern Times* is that America—*Modern Times* is the factory—"modern times" is the assembly line; "modern times" is industrialization, standardization, efficiency—the dehumanizing bureaucratization of all experience. But he is also critiquing Ford's America by parodying life in the factory as a place where work is reduced to a caricature of its most meaninglessly repeated actions. This is what is at once comical and terrifying about the first character we see in *Modern Times*: the Capitalist president-boss. He is seen busying himself with a puzzle, gets bored with it and then picks up the newspaper featuring his "funnies." His "reading" of the newspaper, which features a Tarzan comic on its back page, visible to the audience, *is* the joke and anticipates the action that ensues; the crucial moment in this opening scene is the shift of the president's attention. His intellectual grasp of the world shifts, first from the puzzle (of life), then to the purported objective, broad, "factual" newspaper reportage of the times (which we know to be heavily coloured by the ideology of the day), and finally to the subjective, reductionist, clichéd comic strip. The Tarzan comic that concludes the newspaper represents a reductionist vision of human relationships; the shift in the boss's attention from puzzle of the world to the "objective reality" of the news to clichéd reality of the comic strip. *Modern Times* is structured around shifts from the hard objective reality of life in the industrial age to its clichéd, comic reality—and the agent of this transformation is the factory. It is constructed by shifts in our perception of the familiar and the predictable expectations in and about everyday life dominated by productive work, to the unexpected comic failures of ineptitude in the face of conformity. *Modern Times*, then, documents the mechanization of the public realm—the standardization of human behaviour and interaction through industrialization for the sake of efficiency and profit—and the comic farce this reductionist version of human relationships produces for the audience (Figure 1.1).

The Capitalist-owner boss's function is singular: to increase the speed of the means of production at all costs. But the Tramp can't escape the assembly line that he seems to have put his faith in—he has a hard time keeping up with his own body.

The order imposed on the workers on the assembly line as well as the absurd order forced on the Tramp by the inventor of the mechanical feeding machine will become the subject of a problem—of conflict—that each episode in *Modern Times* will expound upon and that the Tramp reacts to and embodies in his life within "modern times." These early, opening scenes foreground the many gags that Chaplin introduces throughout the film, especially in its semi- final act in the café which features the last employment of the Tramp as a singing waiter, where Chaplin gives himself a voice—a language. The Tramp's transformation at the end of *Modern Times* is the apocalypse of "his" time, and then, he will move on, but in doing so, he will enter post-modern time—time after *Modern Times*—with the gamine.[3] Chaplin will never again use the Tramp as a character—he truly is a child of his age who can speak only in tongues in the coming post-modern world of "talkies."

The "busyness" of the factory assembly line is immediately countered with the sedate interior of the factory boss's impersonal office. His authority looms everywhere—even the sacrosanct privacy of the washroom to which the Tramp escapes to have an unauthorized smoke-break is subject to his surveillance—and he exercises it with detached and disinterested demands. Ironically, his authoritarian demands belie the fact that he is also a nervous wreck without his drugs. On the one hand, the mechanization of the factory, with its assembly lines and commoditized time, is embedded in his language—his directives are mostly commands with numbers—more speed begets more production—directives which are mediated by screens on which he appears as an imposing projection, echoing those of the recorded salesman of the feeding machine. On the other hand, he is human. Time seems to weigh on him like a burden. He first appears to us ingesting pills that his secretary brings to him. His role in life is confined to just one: increase the speed and rate of creating products by controlling the means of production which dominate his assembly line workers.

And this is where we encounter the Tramp in his first role in *Modern Times*. He will fulfil many other roles before reaching that final tableaux he is famous for: walking off towards the horizon on a divided highway with the gamine. Industrialized, mechanized and standardized modern experience—*Modern Times*[4]—will fracture his identity. His pursuit of happiness in this modern life of mechanical reproducibility will cause him to become a mental patient, a criminal, a shipyard worker, a night watchman and, finally, a singing waiter. He will fail at all these roles as the roles will constantly fail him. On the other hand, his fate is that of the Tramp—a homeless man who belongs nowhere—a role he resumes upon release from the asylum.[5]

According to Chaplin, it was a combination of a meeting with Paulette Goddard and a visit to Detroit ("Motor City") that inspired the making of *Modern Times*:

> Paulette struck me as being somewhat of a *gamine*.[6] This would be a wonderful quality for me to get on screen. I could imagine us meeting in a crowded patrol wagon, the tramp and his gamine, and the tramp being very gallant and offering her his seat. This was the basis on which I could build plot and sundry gags.
>
> Then I remembered an interview I had with a bright young reporter on the New York *World*. Hearing that I was visiting Detroit, he had told me of the factory-belt system there—a harrowing story of big industry luring healthy young men off farms who, after four or five years at the belt system, became nervous wrecks.
>
> It was that conversation that gave me the idea for *Modern Times*.
> (377–378)

Clearly, Chaplin's "shirtless" turbine operator who obeys—even salutes—his "president" is a reference to a lost time. This worker, taken "off farms," is condemned to crunch the numbers his employer feeds him. And Chaplin's choice of the feminine "gamine" for the role that Paulette Goddard will play cannot be overstated—it is central to what will become a redeeming love story:

> A remarkable and revealing note by Chaplin on the characterization in *Modern Times* shows that he did not intend the Tramp and the Waif—"the Gamin" as she was called, though in later years Chaplin was inclined to correct this to "Gamine"—as either rebels or victims. They were rather spiritual escapees from a world in which he saw no other hope.
> (Robinson 459)

Moreover, the meaning of Chaplin's *Modern Times* becomes painfully clear as it catches up with the couple in the end, especially the "gamine": "Look into the faces of the masses in our large cities and you will see harassed, defeated souls and in the eyes of most of them weary despair": "nervous wrecks" (*A Comedian Sees the World* 135).

The image, idea and initial presentation of the "Billows Feeding Machine" is the singular event that stands out at the beginning of *Modern Times*.[7] Its sole purpose and design is the elimination of "unproductive" time and the factory worker's lunch hour in particular. The sales pitch: "Don't stop for lunch. Be ahead of your competitor. The Billows feeding machine will eliminate the lunch hour, increase your production and decrease your overhead." Chaplin here stages a perversion of the most basic human need and function in order to reveal the mechanized and indifferent reality of modern times epitomized by the "Corporation." And by building the scene around a basic human need and a foundational social ritual—breaking bread together—he draws our attention to the human condition: *individuals* with the same needs strap the Tramp into the feeding machine—*individuals* operate it—and operate the system that abuses. When it breaks down, it is the assistant—an *individual*—who tries to repair the dehumanizing device, showing more care towards the machine than he does the *individual*, the Tramp who is violated by it. It is clear that the mechanical feeding machine is more than the symbol of these times, but actually the mechanized and vicious embodiment of them; and this is terrifyingly shown by the absent mechanical salesman, whose recording one of the already "defeated—[disembodied]—souls" dressed all in black plays for the boss: a tedious and monotonous voice recording *speaks for the absent salesman/inventor*. Another way to see this image of a disembodied voice is through the artificial intelligence of the machine; from this viewpoint, the machine speaks for itself—we recall Marshall McLuhan's famous dictum, "the medium is the message." Nonetheless, the mechanical salesman's polarizing "mute" and "mediated" sales pitch anticipates Chaplin's emphasis in his next film on the use of speech to dehumanize people in *The Great Dictator*, as well as foreshadowing the gibberish the Tramp gives voice to near the end of the movie. The disembodied voice of the salesman/inventor, mediated through a phonograph record, is laughable. The president, however, is curious and lets the demonstration play itself out. The Tramp is unable to maintain his distance—he is "voluntold" by the boss. The mechanical feeding machine has been described by the recording of the absent salesman/inventor as "state of the *art*"; yet, the macabre irony is that it represents the *machinery* of the entire society the Tramp faces. While the machine force-feeds the Tramp, it is up to the employer to regulate and feed the machine. The faster it "works," the more quickly it comes apart. The Tramp ingests the nuts and bolts that are placed on its feeding tray while an assistant hurries to make repairs. In an ironic turn, the Capitalist-president and potential client-buyer turn away and reject the machine: "It's no good." His response is used as the punch line of the joke, but its meaning is both consistent and sinister—the boss says the machine is "no good" not because it is dehumanizing, but because it doesn't work—it doesn't produce the increase in productivity its sales pitch promised, but the exact opposite—it causes inefficient chaos. For him, it is a disappointment because it doesn't save time but wastes it. Once again, his sudden shift in attention stands out and illuminates the inhumane values of assembly line production. Moments later, he broadcasts his own projected, disembodied order to ramp up the speed of production, which finally causes the Tramp to go berserk, putting his co-workers who have to "rescue" him in peril.

The time-saving and standardization of work that the factory's CEO/president/boss and both the mechanized feeding machine and its cadre of assistants demonstrate is that the Tramp—an ordinary factory worker—cannot be "incorporated." Neither can the Capitalist-owner-president, for that matter, since he is the person who runs the machinery and dictates its use. In this regard, the "mechanical salesman" is the Capitalist's double: the recorded, disembodied voice that speaks for him is similar to the Capitalist-corporate-owner-president's monosyllabic discourse that commands the machinery and by extension its workers in the factory, mediated by

Figure 1.1 The president with his Tarzan comic

8 Work

Figure 1.2 The Tramp strapped in the feeding machine

broadcast screens and aggressive disembodied demands. The mechanical salesman's voice foregrounds speech as the prime tool of corporate industrialized America, a form of authoritarianism that Chaplin can't imagine anyone wanting to be a part of or having a part in (Figure 1.2).

Richard Schickel points out that the "famous eating-machine" sequence is "funny for a while, but it's also visibly an imported comic device." Moreover, "it is an imposition on the film," he writes because "we don't for a minute believe that it is a valid comment on 'modern times'" (26). But that is exactly the point. The joke is too absurd to "impose." That's the *candid* joke. The violence the Tramp experiences causes him to internalize the machine and to act like a machine towards his co-workers in turn. This is Chaplin's only mention of the feeding machine in his autobiography:

> I used a feeding machine as a time-saving device, so that the workers could continue working during the lunch time. The factory sequence resolved itself in the tramp having a nervous breakdown. The plot developed out of the natural sequence of events. After his cure, he gets arrested and meets a *gamine* who has also been arrested for stealing bread. They meet in a police patrol car packed with offenders. From

then on, the theme is about two nondescripts trying to get along in modern times. They are involved in the Depression, strikes, riots and unemployment. Paulette was dressed in rags. She almost wept when I put smudges on her face to make her look dirty. "Those smudges are beauty spots," I insisted.

(378)

Chaplin refers to the Tramp and gamine as "two live spirits in a world of automatons"; as "two live playmates—partners in crime, comrades, babes in the woods" (Robinson 459), but it is his description here of them both as "nondescripts" that is the most revealing since the literal definition of the term means "belonging or appearing to belong to no particular class or kind: not easily described" (Merriam-Webster). The gamine reaffirms their alienation and disenfranchisement midway through the film when, in answer to the Tramp's question, "Where do you live?" she says: "No place—anywhere." The entire film fills the gap between Chaplin's first and second sentence: "I used a feeding machine as a time-saving device, so that the workers could continue working during the lunch time. The factory sequence resolved itself in the tramp having a nervous breakdown." Chaplin's own remarks, then, force us to look at the automated feeding machine more closely. Not only does the machine turn against man but it also reverses and revises a myth implicit in the majority of the criticism of the film that views the Tramp a kind of heroic underdog or David who fights and defeats a Goliath:

> Machinery that gives abundance has left us in want. Our knowledge has made us cynical; our cleverness, hard and unkind. We think too much and feel too little. More than machinery we need humanity. More than cleverness, we need kindness and gentleness. Without these qualities, life will be violent and all will be lost.
>
> (*My Autobiography* 394)

The fact of the matter is, it is Goliath who devours the Tramp and "nondescripts" like him. The Tramp survives modern times, he does not erase or elide, much less defeat them. And he certainly does not transcend or master them as a few critics have suggested. His "half-smile" at the end of the film (he literally "puts it on" with a hand gesture that begins in the middle of his mouth and ends on one of his cheeks) is merely another nervous and ambiguous gesture—a pretence, an imitation—potentially a dissimulation. Contrast this with Joker's smile as he rises above the herd. Arthur Fleck's "smile" is written in blood—it's real (in real time)—it covers his whole face cheek to cheek and he is ready to face the maelstrom. The Tramp's half-smile at the end of the film, though contrived, is still "wincingly naïve" (Ross 20); Fleck's *cum* Joker's is the "real life" spectacle of our post-modern times.

By lunch time in his first scene, the Tramp is already showing signs of a breakdown. He is wound up and cannot seem to wind down. The working hours show themselves on his countenance and comportment—his expressions and gestures. He is also becoming predacious. When the "Whistle Stops" and the assembly line halts production he can't do anything other than repeat the gestures of work—he continues tightening the metal nuts and bolts out of the air, even misconstruing the decorative buttons on the secretary's dress as she passes by him for fasteners which he then tries to tighten. These "movements" and gestures advance the plot—they are the visual joke within the joke—and anticipate what comes next in logical fashion: spilling soup on his colleague because the machine winds him up and he cannot wind down, the attack of the killer mechanical feeding machine and, finally, the Tramp attacking his co-workers in a psychotic outburst before being taken away to the mental hospital.

> The jerky movements of Chaplin's body do not simply *repeat* the movement of the assembly line but they mimic it, that is, they share in it, extend it, and thereby *master* it. For the movement of the assembly line, when taken over by Chaplin's body, is turned into a choreography with a beauty of its own.
>
> (Symons 143–144)

He "masters it" to the extent that he "becomes it." This is not at all that beautiful from a post-modern point of view, as *Joker* will demonstrate.

These "accidents" on the assembly line foreshadow the violence unleashed by the feeding machine just as the feeding machine feeds off of and even anticipates the Tramp's behaviour and passive acquiescence; it breaks down, too, and runs amok. For a moment, however, it gives the Tramp exactly what he wants: food and confinement. And the Tramp is more than willing to take what it dishes out. The machine, doing what it is designed to do, feeds him even the metal nuts that the assistant casually sets aside. Even good manners are programmed, which the machine maintains even as it implodes—an absurd situation—not unlike the Tramp who seems gentle, bumbling, but well-mannered also—"polite." And he performs this and shows it each time he tips his hat to inanimate things, for example, with an almost complete indifference to them. The "doubleness" of the figure of the Tramp is always in front of us, which bears on Eisenstein seeing in these films "dissonance," "conflict" and the seeds of "montage construction." What does or should the viewer think when this *problematic* character becomes the centre of the film? We think: Who is this figure? Why are things happening to him? His figure raises riddles for the viewer and the "viewed": about what we are watching and whether to believe in him or not. What is both unsettling and unnerving is how everything returns to "normal" nonetheless. But normal also means speed, and no sooner is the Tramp free of the destructive machine than new directives are announced: "Speed her up." It's only going to get worse. The idea of efficiency through the standardization introduced by industrialization produces not only assembly lines but also violence.[8] But here he has no choice—he's strapped in and confined. The mechanical feeding machine not only violates; it is the Tramp's first lesson on how to violate.

The psychiatrist R.D. Laing understood that the root of mental illness is societal and existential; the social pressures of one's lived experience—the social pressures of industrialization in the Tramp's experience—could be more or less troubling than one's symptoms. The implications are profound especially once we distinguish between modern and post-modern times. The Tramp is deemed "crazy" by his co-workers. But it is Arthur Fleck at the beginning of the film *Joker* who asks his psychiatrist the relevant question of post-modern times: "Is it just me or is it getting crazier out there?" *Modern Times* grafts the violence of modern times onto the character of the Tramp, but unlike the Tramp, Arthur Fleck understands that his present time is itself "violent." The violence resides outside of Fleck, and he internalizes it; in *Modern Times*, it continues to reside outside the Tramp's seemingly playful, seemingly innocent "naiveté"—he merely seeks to benefit by and from it. But this "wincingly naïve" character trait is Chaplin's greatest illusion (Ross 20). Fleck, unreliable narrator that he is, doesn't fool us. He is just pathetic—he makes things up; he is a construction of his time; *Modern Times* on the other hand is a construction of the Tramp/Chaplin, since he does nothing to elide its uncaring and mechanized ethos; and even when he finally speaks, he undermines sense. In sum, Arthur Fleck is a psychotic idealist next to the increasingly indifferent and predacious Tramp. The character and the machine join in one of the culminating images that follows the Tramp's return to the line.

When the Tramp is sent back to the assembly line, the enhanced new quota of tightening the metal nuts and bolts causes him to go berserk—he runs amok. Eat or be eaten, which is exactly what happens in the next episode in one of the film's most iconic montage sequences, in which the Tramp is swallowed by the machine. The machine and machinery that consumes the Tramp depersonalizes the "mute salesman." His interaction with the president in his office is itself a form of montage in which the juxtaposition of recorded speech speaks along with the demonstrator-character's actions. The Capitalist-owner-boss listens with his eyes; in this moment, he seems to mimic the spectator's act of perception. These self-reflexive images bring us back to the film as form—even sensual form—making us aware that we are in a kind of factory ourselves—perhaps a cinema—watching the film's projected and mechanically reproduced images running in our very presence—in the present tense no less. "Mechanical reproduction," as Walter Benjamin points out in his seminal essay, "is inherent in the very technique of film production" (*Illuminations* 223).[9] And, as we have already noted, the most astonishing accomplishment of the film is that it uses the very technologies and techniques of mechanization and standardization of the machine age (the spooling of still images through sets of gears to create the illusion of both movement and time) to create a facsimile of a life lived in the pathos of modernist reality—"a fearful symmetry." To elaborate: the machine that gorges the Tramp shifts the spectator's attention once more; moreover, this shift in perception is reinforced by the Tramp's own actions as he continues to "work." The Tramp, unlike his co-workers—unlike the spectator—does not notice any shift. For a moment, the scene "shifts attention away from assertions of power to the instrument through which that power is exercised" (Morrison np): the machine. But the machine is also the camera and, therefore, implicates the spectator in the act of seeing which it constructs. Just to reinforce the metaphor, the machine can be run backwards, reversing time like a film projector as it eventually returns the Tramp to his workplace.

It can be argued that in his state of unfocused awareness, the Tramp is ignorant. But the word ignorant also opens up a way of seeing the scene. In fact, he might be less innocent than ignorant. The artist and film maker Vera Frenkel sees ignorance as a probe:

> There is a kind of ignorance that can be called benign: a state arrived at by travelling through knowledge to the other side. I'd use the word "innocence" if it had fewer connotations of pre-pubescent passivity. True innocence is knowing and seductive in non-temporal ways—ask any pederast—but the word doesn't give us that. It suggests only an unearned purity, prior to the effect of events. I find more interesting what Hamada calls "the second spring," a renewed freshness of vision arrived at only after travelling once through the seasons. I am calling this special state "benign ignorance."
>
> (27)

We are able to see into the machine and machinery of *Modern Times*:

> The shift of perception and the upheaval caused by letting go of the known world for a time can give rise to a discovery. That discovery or way of seeing differently is often confused with newness or originality. But we invent what is already there.
>
> (28)

Arthur Fleck, on the other hand, sees "what is already there" all too clearly. He laughs as compulsively and uncontrollably as the Tramp continues to mime his gestures when and where they are no longer "appropriate."

From the standpoint of the disembodied Arthur Fleck ("All I have are negative thoughts"), the Tramp's reactions are anything but innocent; yet, from the vantage point of industrialized society, his rejoinder is the norm—sucked into the machine he continues to do his job—he is compliant. Fleck, too, goes into the machine the moment he steps into his refrigerator and closes the door. But his intent is to fortify himself against the coming cold. The machinery in *Modern Times* consumes as much as it produces; its common denominator is the production of naive, self-involved, dreamy consumers in the pursuit of their own narcissistic comfortable existence and "happiness." The "modern" social reality that the Tramp experiences is increasingly an extension of the machine. The Tramp's "actions" after he has been regurgitated by it transform the factory into a "jungle." The word, which originally meant "uncultivated ground," takes on its secondary meaning in this scene, which becomes "a place notoriously lawless and violent"—a "hobo camp." And the Tramp's gestures are an imitation of this transforming context—with each incident, the Tramp becomes more and more unhinged; the machine dehumanizes the Tramp and induces panic; he brandishes wrenches in both hands above his head in imitation of the Greek god Pan—the god of the wild. He chases after two women, inside and outside of the factory, once again confusing the decorative fasteners that adorn their dresses for nuts and bolts that require his immediate attention. He resists being caught by a policeman who comes to the rescue of a "woman with buttoned bosom."[10] Upon entering the factory, we notice that he punches his time card—this detail is comical—but it also registers his re-entry back into the machinery of industrialized society, work and labour. To put it plainly, then, the Tramp is dehumanized by a machine, put back to work, forced to increase production, experiences a mental breakdown and proceeds to cause a riot inside the factory in which he is the only "wrench in the works" so to speak. Let loose, he chases and cavorts about, even leaping onto a large iron metal hook and chain from which he dangles, bringing us back to the Tarzan image from earlier and putting the president of the corporation—along with everyone else—into a comic situation depicted in his newspaper "funnies" only moments ago—welcome to the jungle—except the Tramp is no "noble savage."[11]

If conflict and collision is the nerve of cinematic art as Sergei Eisenstein asserts, then the workers' protest that occurs in the street is a perfect illustration, but Chaplin films the collision his own way.[12] Three passages from Chaplin's autobiography illuminate his aesthetic—these crucial statements stand out for our purposes here. The first passage reads:

> Personally, I loathe tricky effects, photographing through the fireplace from the viewpoint of a piece of coal, or travelling with an actor through a hotel lobby as though escorting him on a bicycle; to me they are facile and obvious. As long as an audience is familiar with the set, it does not want the tedium of a travelling smear across the screen to see an actor move from one place to another. Such pompous effects slow up action, are boring and unpleasant, and have been mistaken for that tiresome word "art."
>
> My own camera set-up is based on facilitating choreography for the actor's movements. When a camera is placed on the floor or moves about the player's nostrils, it is the camera that is giving the performance and not the actor. The camera should not obtrude.
>
> Time-saving in films is still the basic virtue. Both Eisenstein and Griffith knew it. Quick cutting and dissolving from one scene to another are the dynamics of film technique.
>
> (*My Autobiography* 250)

The second passage highlights an exchange between Chaplin and the modern American writer Gertrude Stein:

> She theorized about cinema plots. "They are too hackneyed, complicated and contrived." She would like to see me in a movie just walking up the street and turning a corner, then another corner, and another. I thought of saying that her idea was a paraphrase of that mystic emphasis of hers: "Rose is a rose is a rose"—but an instinct stopped me.
>
> (302)

The third passage succinctly sums up Chaplin's political vision as it relates to his art and *Modern Times*:

> Before the opening of *Modern Times* a few columnists wrote that they had heard rumours the picture was communistic. I suppose this was because of a summary of the story that had already appeared in the Press. However, the liberal reviewers wrote that it was neither for nor against communism and that metaphorically I had sat on the fence.
>
> (378)

Each of the three statements illuminate the episodes that follow the Tramp's release from an asylum; he stumbles twice as he exits the asylum putting the lie to the intertitle's first announcement that he is "Cured of a nervous breakdown but without a job"; he "leaves the hospital to start life anew." We will take the film's advice and begin "anew"—although the title cards might be a form of unreliable narrator; the three passages from Chaplin's text—in his own words—fit the "liberty or death" protest demonstration sequence that follows beautifully.

The scene is "comoedic"—the figures undergo trials and endurance. Each scene depicts the Tramp's entanglement in the world of "modern times," not unlike Dante's *Divine Comedy*, "a place of sterile barbarity, remote from all true civilization."[13] It shows that the human condition is "conditional." The scene lasts only two minutes; two minutes to set up and show conflict; two minutes to set up and show collision; two minutes to set up and show the Tramp getting into trouble and getting out of it; the life of the street goes on around him. "Take it easy and try to avoid excitement," we recall his discharging doctor's advice. And with that advice, the Tramp is "Cured of a nervous breakdown but without a job, he leaves the hospital to start life anew"—"liberated" once more from a system which washes its hands of him. Two minutes to set up the next scene that is based on the doctor's injunctions and advice which are a clearly ironic foreshadowing, since neither the Tramp nor his environment is stable (except Chaplin's camera that records them from "outside").

From the hospital, the Tramp descends into the urban life of his times—the stumbles he takes are a clear sign that he is unimproved—and the palimpsest of montage images of the hustle and bustle of the street and its noise show his circumstances haven't improved at all. In the first scene, there is the sensibility of a Cubist aesthetic in the way Chaplin "stages" it. The figure is perceived in a ground, hence his emphasis on the word "familiarity" in his meditation on the reciprocal figure–ground relationship that is filmed from a measured distance that constructs and enlarges (broadens) our "familiarity" with (and hence knowledge of) the overall picture, which Chaplin foregrounds in the first passage:

> Personally, I loathe tricky effects.

Here, Chaplin emphasizes "quick cutting," which he also defines as "simple cutting"[14]:

> My own camera set-up is based on facilitating choreography for the actor's movements. When a camera is placed on the floor or moves about the player's nostrils, it is the camera that is giving the performance and not the actor. The camera should not obtrude.
>
> Time-saving in films is still the basic virtue.
>   (*My Autobiography* 250)

In an interview with Richard Meryman, Chaplin asserts:

Trick cutting doesn't interest me because I'm so much interested in the human equation, and not photographing a stone or a drop of blood falling on it. I suppose there is merit in the accumulation of what the effect will be, but I don't make pictures that way.

(362)

Time-saving is also tied to Chaplin's spatial construction of the scenes. He saves a great deal of it in constructing a concise narrative by simply filming the Tramp as he walks from one point to the next; out of a door and towards a street corner. The screen is suffused with a montage of spectacles and of street cars, rescue vehicles, crowds and construction. The images engulf us since they fill the screen and cause us to remember where we have been and what we have previously seen (at a distance). The earlier metaphors and images of herded sheep fading into crowds of people, presumably on their way to work, are now a literal (unsentimental) montage of city tropes. Such tropes are keys to the narrative structure of the film and function like intertitles. Chaplin aims his camera at the Tramp who is haplessly stumbling along, casting his eye down to acknowledge the source of his stumble (a broken sidewalk before a closed factory) and back up again to survey the scenes around him—the set. The Tramp's familiar gestures direct, familiarize and punctuate the spectator's eye which also reads: he looks, we see. Chaplin's insistence on the audience's familiarity with the set is a balancing act of sorts that the Tramp's interactions expose—although we move along with him in parallel fashion, our distance is secure. He sees only what is in front of him now. In the time it has taken him to walk from the asylum to the corner, we are reminded of where we are—we see through the Tramp's eyes as he looks and surveys—his vision guides our own—but from a measured distance. Thus, "familiarity" carries two meanings in the way Chaplin is using it here: the normalizing of the "audience" as passive viewers of mere entertainment and the aesthetics of "familiarity" or "de-familiarity"—the making strange of familiar actions and things in order to hold the attention of "informed spectators" of the whole film and not just identifying with the figure of "The Tramp" who of course dominates all the scenes as the audience's double: the "naïve observer."

Chaplin's "direction" is closer to a curation in which he uses the language of film montage and direct observation to bring us back to and situate us in a precise moment of time: the larger historical context of the great depression. Chaplin, here, is stark (complete) and unvarnished, like a documentary film-maker. One word, the sign attached to a locked and boarded-up factory door sums the historical situation up: "Closed." Once more, Chaplin reminds us that "The characteristics of the film lie not only in the manner in which man presents himself to mechanical equipment but also in the manner in which, by means of this apparatus, man can represent his environment" (*Illuminations* 187). A "familiar" set-up, for Chaplin, "is aesthetically legitimate to the extent that it evokes the illusion of actuality. [By] the same token," as Kracauer observes, "anything stagy is uncinematic"—("tricky effects")—"if it passes over the basic properties of the medium" (60). The passages highlighted previously from Chaplin's autobiography clarify the distinction Kracauer makes between "the illusion of actuality" and "stagy, uncinematic effects"—nothing must detract from the picture's candid realism. Informed by these basic aesthetic principles, Chaplin, the director, frames *Modern Times*. And as we will see, director Todd Phillips, 86 years later in *Joker*, makes sure that there is no passing over "the basic properties of the medium." As Phillips reminds us, "I think you'd have to watch *Modern Times* because we believe there is some Chaplin in Arthur [Fleck] that I think is really important"[15]—just as there is a presence of Gertrude Stein's and cubism's aesthetic in the way Chaplin constructs scenes.

In setting up what comes next, as referenced in the second passage, Chaplin refers to—and seems to respond to—Gertrude Stein's question, giving her what she wants to see.

From the street corner where the Tramp stands we can see the waterfront—a view that foreshadows the "gamine" character—"a child of the waterfront." There is nothing "too hackneyed, complicated and contrived" about that. Situations always develop from familiar, ordinary and commonplace occurrences and experiences. And no sooner do we find our familiar bearings than a construction lorry turns a corner from the opposite side of the street; it passes the Tramp whose eye follows it; the camera takes us along for the ride now, and we are looking back at the Tramp from the flatbed of the lorry, stacked with boards from which a caution flag extends. Again, there is nothing "complicated and contrived" here. But this scene illuminates Chaplin's emphasis on the gag in relation to the whole film. "I was beginning to think of comedy in a structural sense," he writes, "and to become conscious of its architectural form. Each sequence implied the next sequence, all of them relating to the whole" (*My Autobiography* 208). This scene becomes the site of both confusion and fate and follows the montage of images that have reintroduced the Tramp to modern life—images that are double exposed—one on top of the other—of cars, crowds, jack hammers, trollies and emergency vehicles—paradigmatically, but the lost flag scene develops in a syntagmatic fashion. Chaplin shifts attention from the psychologically charged montage images *of* the chaotic street to a narrative of events *in* the street. Chaplin emphasizes, depicts and gives us, in his own clear words and gestures, "the situation." "If you get a good comedy situation it goes on and on and has many radiations" (Meryman 361). Gertrude Stein might have been impressed.

Many critics of *Modern Times* assume the flag in this scene to be "red." Flags under these conditions of revolt, unionism, militancy, socialism, communism and agitation would be "emblematic" of the chaotic situation of "modern times." That seemingly innocent assumption, however, oversimplifies the visual experience of this object in a black and white film. That assumption is misplaced, just like the flag itself which will soon become displaced, fall to the ground and be noticed by the Tramp, who attempts to intervene, attempting to signal its loss to the driver of the truck. If we identify the flag as "red" it is purely out of convention—retrospectively and simplistically in alignment with the context of what comes next in the film. But the scene plays with our assumptions and expectations in a work of art that is built up scene by scene and fragment by fragment; Chaplin's insistence is always on a sequence in which seeing is a verb: "If a gag interfered with the logic of events, no matter how funny it was, I would not use it" (*My Autobiography* 208). Quick and sudden changes in this scene force our attention to shift. If we look closely enough, we see the string that holds the flag in place until the precise moment in the film for it to be released—catching the attention and initiating the reaction of the Tramp who has his eye already on it. No "tricky effect," that—only a gesture—a quick shift in context—that constructs new paradigms and possibilities; in fact, the scene's "set-up" is almost pedestrian. The camera simply records one object's fall from another, then the human reactions this accident initiates, "appropriate" or not as determined by circumstantial context(s).

In Chaplin's view, the "pompous effects" available to the medium makes film "boring and unpleasant"—"tiresome art." Yet, the scene in the street with the flag is one of Chaplin's most profound narrative sequences. "Everything is there for the action" and confusion that takes place.[16] Chaplin's image of the string holding the flag in place, then accidentally breaking, illustrates that life happens beyond our control. Soon the comic will reveal the fate and destiny of the character before the character realizes what is happening around him. But the audience sees something the Tramp does not—the revolutionary mob gathering behind him as he runs after the truck, waving the flag to alert the driver to the accident that has just occurred. The Tramp's "artlessness"—his word—in this scene is the director Chaplin's choice; in contrast to the comedian Arthur Fleck who is consistently depicted by Phillips as pathetic and naturally unfunny in his craft. In fact, the Tramp's artlessness contributes to his absurd situations and makes them more realistic and almost surreal—"ordinary" and uncanny. So much of the scene with the flag is set up by the Tramp's looking about and then focusing on the immediate; he is depicted as looking at life, not art. But he's doing so in a work of art—a spectator being watched.

Here, we return to the third passage referenced in Chaplin's autobiography, which addresses itself to Chaplin's politics in relation to his critics: "Before the opening of *Modern Times* a few columnists wrote that they had heard rumours the picture was communistic" (378). He is neither "liberal" nor "communistic" in *Modern Times*; moreover, his political frame of reference in the film is clear—expressed in rigorously candid terms: he is concerned about humanity and what the machinery of modern times does to our collective, common good; not to mention its disastrous consequences for the individual *in* and *of* modern times. His feelings towards modern America as a beacon of hope are equally clear: "Somehow I feel that in America lies the hope of the whole world. For whatever takes place in the transition of this epoch-making time, America will be equal to it" (*A Comedian Sees the World* 144). *Modern Times* is the transitional film for Chaplin and, as we will see, for the Tramp himself.

Despite Chaplin's clarity in his art, the subject of Chaplin's politics is a much debated one. We must once more defer to the auteur himself: "I don't want to create a revolution—I just want to create a few more films."[17] This insight must serve as a critical caveat because the narrative sequence initiated by the flag that falls off the construction lorry's load is more about the way circumstance creates the character of the Tramp—he is made and recreated by his surroundings in the scene. The emphasis here is quite intentionally on how the *situation* creates the "hero." "[You] cannot be funny without a funny situation," Chaplin points out. "You can do something clownish, perhaps stumble, but you must have a funny situation" (Meryman 361). This reminds us of Chaplin's emphasis on familiarity as the foundational element of all comedy: "You have an absurd situation, and you treat it with a complete reality. And the audience knows it, so they're in the spirit. It's so real to them and it's so absurd, it gives them exultation" ("Meryman 362").

Chaplin's comments make it clear that he is critically aware of and responsive to the political conditions and controversies and puts to rest that the film as a work of art is neither communist, socialist, nor anti-communist—these words impose a limitation on the film. Moreover, Chaplin's statement opens up the multiple meanings of the flag that the Tramp finds in the street: "I'm not touting for any ideology or any schism that exists" (*Charlie Chaplin: Interviews* 110). Chaplin is caught by these presuppositions of the critics in the political vice of the ideological hopes and positions of the times by being labelled "communist," accused of being a left-wing agitator, because of the purported "meanings" of his films. Rather, Chaplin sets out to perform a parody of the agitator in a system that demeans and dehumanizes the individual; and, in *Modern Times*, the emphasis is always on the destructive socio-economic effects of industrialization, against the dehumanization of which no ideology of his day has provided an effective antidote. The film shows throughout the struggle of the character against being demeaned and is nevertheless consistently cast aside. *Modern Times* becomes, then, as acerbic a critique of socialism, as his next film, *The Great Dictator*, becomes an acerbic critique of fascism. Both systems are, of course, absurd—comically inhumane to Chaplin, which we can see most clearly in the observation that on seeing the famous Leni Riefenstahl film *The Triumph of the Will* (1935), his first and overwhelming reaction was to burst out laughing. It may very well have been his inspiration for both his films *Modern Times* and *The Great Dictator* (1940).

Nonetheless, "In modern life, as in *Modern Times*," as Stephen Weismann comments, "Chaplin's 'sentimental radicalism' would later be interpreted as Communist radicalism by members of the House Un-American Activities Committee (HUAC) during the Cold War and Red scare of the late 1940" (51). But the Tramp never sees himself as revolutionary, much less as subversive, he is only ever mistakenly identified as such by others. "Everything is ready for the action" of which the Tramp is a naïve catalyst who plunges in *medias res* (*A Comedian Sees the World* 106).

So the Tramp, "innocently," rushes out into the street to retrieve the flag; he picks it up and waves it at the receding truck driver in front of him at the precise moment a labour march behind him turns the corner to the left of where he was standing just seconds ago. We see this scene unfold from our privileged vantage point of the truck on which the camera is mounted in the foreground—we are facing the Tramp who reaches out for our (and the driver's) attention. Police on horseback enter the frame, also from the foreground, forcing the protesters to retreat and scatter, which they do in reaction to the aggressive police officers. The Tramp retreats backwards into the crowd which surprises and engulfs him but ends up in a sewer. As he tries to free himself, two officers descend on him, yanking him free with aggressive force—this is the second time the Tramp has been "retrieved"—less than twenty minutes into the film he finds himself inadvertently in a second "riot." The authorities "identify" him as the "leader." He tries his best to explain the situation, but this only compounds the misunderstanding. The point is that he has nothing to do with the protest or its issues but is only implicated by "accident" (Figure 1.3 and Figure 1.4).

Many critics such as Richard Schickel describe the scene this way:

> The little Tramp is ambling along a street when a lumber truck rumbles past him. Boards are sticking out beyond the back end of its open bed. On them is perched a red flag, intended to warn motorists that this load exceeds the truck's limits. The red flag falls off the truck. Chaplin picks it up and begins waving it to the driver to attract his attention so

Figure 1.3 Red flag (long shot)

Figure 1.4 Red flag (close-up)

he can return it.[18] As he does so, a Communist demonstration, its members shouting slogans and waving similar flags, rounds the corner and falls in behind Chaplin. Now he's innocently leading a presumptively revolutionary band. A police riot squad moves in. Heads are busted, arrests are made, and Chaplin ends up in jail for disturbing the peace. In its simultaneous economy and richness, this is one of Chaplin's most supreme moments, a gag as classic as any he had perpetuated twenty years earlier. I also think it perfectly symbolizes his relationship to left-wing politics—innocently supportive of communism but scarcely a devoted ideologue.

(27)

The scene is actually less about Chaplin's politics than it is about his aesthetics and film-making.

The flag falling off the truck cargo and ending up, purely by chance, in the hands of the Tramp has further implications. Making the assumption that the flag is "red" in a black and white film is, of course (in the mind of the director), what the audience is "expected" to bring to the scene—if only because traffic law requires dangerous cargoes to be so red-flagged, and "everyone knows this." It is equally true that the film-maker expects the audience to also make the political connection of that flag to the red ensign of the communist international movement—or, if they think the flag might be black (it appears to be in the black and white movie), as the ensign of the (contemporary) anarchist revolutionary movement. These revolutionary movements were "modern" anti-capitalist ideologies embraced by many workers of the world at the time the film was made and most particularly of unionised workers during the *Modern Times* of the worldwide depression of the 1930s—workers which are a subject or component or class of the film (but by no means its only subject, component or class).

However, the focus of the director, the "gag" or "joke" of the scene, if you will, is that the string that attaches the flag to the lorry load breaks. What the scene "signifies" here is not whether the flag's "colour" is "understood" (taken for granted) by the audience, but that *any* flag acquires meaning only by what or to whom that piece of fabric is perceived to be attached. Attached to a lorry load, it is a warning—a danger sign—a device that keeps people safe and away from harm. Attached to the perceived leader of a herd of angry, unemployed workers, that flag signifies the opposite—the intent to do revolutionary harm to others, of the threat of blood being spilled in the cause of fighting a perceived social injustice—a threat, moreover, that is fulfilled in a subsequent scene involving the gamine's father. But attached to an "innocent" bystander, it means nothing. And therein lies the film-maker's intended comedy: the audience watching the film, being objectively outside of its characters and actions, becomes involved in a conspiratorial (albeit manipulated) relationship with the film-maker, recognizing that it's not the flag that's at issue in the film at all, but what it is (mis)taken to signify *by some of the characters of the film*. If it's attached to a "nobody," signifying "nothing" but detached concern, the flag means—*nothing*. That's the joke. And prior to both World War II and the Cold War (i.e., in 1935–1936 when the film was made and released), what was going on in the world, politically and ideologically, *in the Modern Times of its day*, could be seen by the film-maker and the audience as nothing more (or less!) than a cynical joke. The Tramp is pulled out of a sewer he's fallen into still holding the flag at the end of the episode.[19]

Accidents have consequences. The police patrol car the Tramp is thrown into faces in the direction of the asylum from which he's just been released only moments before. This will be a familiar road for the Tramp who is taken to jail for the first time in the film. The scene in the street with the flag is significant because it shows that the Tramp lives by trial and error, and this "error" on the part of the "authorities"—of thinking that he is part of the protest—sets in motion almost limitless patterns of action and behaviour in the film.

The next sequence introduces the film's second "principal character"—"a gamin." Again, the scene lasts just over two minutes. We see her first living up to her name—"a child of the waterfront who refuses to go hungry"— stealing bananas which she tosses to other children who see her. Yet, she is not just any "child of the waterfront," but one that "refuses to go hungry." That's important, because, unlike the Tramp who is utterly noncommittal and compliant, even co-operative, she refuses to accept the condition circumstances have put her in.

She is spotted and runs—we witness her in the act of stealing the fruit, tossing bananas to the children who have gathered while also eating and enjoying some of the fruit herself—as we also witness a man who enters the frame and chases after her. With a quick glance away to her right, she makes her escape and defiantly eats one of her stolen bananas, first in full frame, then in close-up in front of the audience. The next scene depicts the interior of her family's sparsely decorated home with its cracked walls and wooden table; her two "little sisters—motherless" play in the doorway with empty tins. She runs over to them with the bananas. Together they are taken aback by the sudden appearance of their father—"one of the unemployed"—and she hurries her sisters out of the room. He approaches, from the "fourth wall" of the spectator (implying he is "one of us"), takes off his black hat, sets it on his small table, drinks a dipper of water and sits down, now facing "us" (the camera). A close-up shot shows his anguish, which the gamin breaks with her surprising and sudden reappearance from another room with the bananas. They embrace and she distributes more of the fruit—to him, her sisters and herself. The scene ends with the gamin sitting on her father's lap eating a banana (next to her two younger sisters). How are we to "see" this? Clearly, this infantilizing image also sexualizes her in a profound way; it singles her out as different from her "little sisters"—and foregrounds and advances the plot.

In this brief scene, the gamin is transformed before our very eyes from a "street urchin"—"a child of the waterfront who refuses to go hungry"—into a "gamine." And this is also where the film takes several darker turns that will be more fully explicated for the audience in subsequent scenes.

It is important that we understand the meaning of the French word "gamin," which has both masculine and feminine connotations depending on how it is spelled. "Gamin" in its masculine form means "street urchin," "orphan" or "kid"; it derives from the verb phrase meaning "to steal." *Modern Times*, in its intertitles and credits, uses the masculine form "gamin" but here is where Paulette Goddard's characterization in the film must be reconsidered. While the film uses "gamin" in the title cards and credits, we must also recall the feminine form of the word— "gamine"—means a "small, slim, pert young girl." Chaplin's biographer, David Robinson, points out that Chaplin "in later life, learned of the problem himself and also decided to include the final e."[20] Robinson's observation is supported by Chaplin's conscious choice to use the feminine form—*gamine*—in his autobiography. The distinction is anything but "pedantic." The Tramp falls in love with the "gamin" who isn't a gamin at all, but his "love interest" in the film. As the "gamine," she is young enough that juvenile officers still go after her, but unlike the way, they treat her two younger sisters, who are immediately taken by the nanny state. This narrative is rigorously upheld in the film: consequently, the Tramp's harbouring of the "gamine" from the law is not only illegal, it remains morally suspect. Clearly, Chaplin wants the audience to be attracted to her in a way that elides the masculine meaning of the word and is closer to the feminine form:

> It is easy to dress an actress attractively in fashionable clothes, but to dress a flower-girl and have her look attractive, as in *City Lights*, was difficult. The girl's costume in *The Gold Rush* was not such a problem. But Paulette's outfit in *Modern Times* required as much thought and finesse as a Dior creation. If a *gamine* [Chaplin's emphasis] costume is treated without care, the patches look theatrical and unconvincing. In dressing an actress as a street urchin or a flower-girl I aimed to create a poetic effect and not to distract from her personality.
>
> (378)

Art imitates life. Paulette Goddard was twenty-six years old in 1936; Chaplin was forty-seven. Chaplin's view of Goddard's character as a gamine rather than gamin is essential for a "correct" reading of the film. Her presence is life-changing for the Tramp and not because she is a child, but because she is a young woman. *Modern Times* is anything but "innocent" of sexuality.

The next scene, which is about the Tramp's new life in prison, begins to establish the film's more prurient and darker thematic: "Held as a communist leader, our innocent victim languishes in jail." But while he may be "innocent as charged" as a "communist leader," having been misidentified and falsely arrested as one, he certainly remains an "innocent victim" of the system. In fact, the only word that bears any semblance of the truth concerning the Tramp's character is the verb "languishes." So now we see him incarcerated by the State, but his own perspective on his confinement stuns and arrests us.

Actually, "languid" describes his interaction and relationship to his sizeable cellmate quite accurately. The Tramp is escorted to his cell only to find his cohabiting prisoner sitting on the bottom bunk, embroidering. In a playful way at first, in any case, Chaplin upsets the conventionally effeminate connotations of the craft which in "modern times" was a skill marking an upper-class girl's passage into womanhood. In depicting the Tramp's cellmate indulging in this pastime, Chaplin suggests a homoerotic relationship between the hapless Tramp languishing as his more "masculine" companion establishes dominance. He looks the new prisoner over and responds with rapid ease to his initial bumbling around on the bunk; he picks him up effortlessly, throws the Tramp against the wall and insists that he take the top bunk. He makes it clear that he prefers the bottom. "Some critics declared that psychology could not be expressed on the silent screen," Chaplin observes, "that obvious action, such as heroes bending ladies over tree-trunks and breathing fervently down into their tonsils, or chair-swinging, knock-out rough stuff, was its only means of expression." *Modern Times* "is full of subtle suggestion" (294–295). This unnerving scene foresees a dangerous liaison. The prevalence of homosexual relations in prisons is a common trope no matter what the times, as Chaplin's audience surely is aware.

But what stands out immediately is the fact that the prison in *Modern Times* is a quiet place—there is silence among the prisoners—they march in single file, forming a line in and out of the cells and cafeteria under the watchful eyes of the guards. It is a place not at all much different from the factory in the film's opening scenes, subject at all times to surveillance and authority. This is a subtle point in the film, and it may derive from Chaplin's earlier experiences of prisons that he visited. "England still has the system of enforced silence among the prisoners," he asserts. "I cannot understand why this has continued. To deprive a man of that most civilizing factor in human society—speech—seems to me unscientific" (*A Comedian Sees the World* 40–41). The prison may illuminate a repressed quietude in this otherwise "noisy" (silent) film that is itself unnerving, but the unspoken violence that Chaplin implies exists inside its walls is forced intimacy and aggression.

The prison environment is another kind of "factory," and we know how the Tramp fared in that environment earlier on. And so is the "asylum." Director Todd Phillips asserts:

> *Modern Times* is about a man who feels he can't keep up with the times. As a result, he decides to just put himself in prison by the film's end. There's a moment in *Joker* where an Arkham State Hospital employee tells Arthur Fleck that sometimes people just admit themselves there when they have nowhere else to go. By the film's end, we see Fleck inside a mental hospital.
>
> (Acuna np)

The "banter" back and forth that consists of looks and stares between the Tramp and his new cellmate continues in the cafeteria—we see them sitting and eating together. In *Modern Times*, the prison takes on all the trappings of the culture of its age; crime does not end there. A third nefarious inmate who just happens to take his seat in the cafeteria next to the Tramp is singled out by two prison authorities and Chaplin's camera frames him in a circle or "point of view" shot. This third actor is dealing cocaine ("nose powder"), and he is about to be found out. As the prison officials approach him, he dispenses with the product by pouring it into a saltshaker which, of course, the Tramp uses to salt his bread and gruel and the sudden hit of drugs transforms him from powerless to powerful, just as the Boss's power derives in part from the drug his secretary "deals" him in his very first appearance in the film.

The structure of the jail cafeteria scene is similar to the previous flag scene on the street during the march. Our attention shifts with the flag—its movement from one context to the next in quick intervals of time; once more, spectators find themselves in a conspiratorial relationship with the cocaine scene, since we know that the "nose powder" that the Tramp's fellow prisoner pours into a saltshaker, which he "innocently" and unknowingly ingests will create a scene—a potentially comical situation for the audience—but also one which puts the Tramp in some danger with his large cellmate: his naiveté once again undermines the danger. Because of the ingestion of the powder, the Tramp unwittingly gains enough strength to escape from his role of subservience, and once again, the scene becomes for the observer a way of seeing: the shifts in perception show not only the comic confusion of roles and expectations but also the spectator's relation to the joke which stands above or outside the law in this displaced perception. The cocaine also alters the Tramp's own perception—its effect allows him to dominate his oversized cellmate. He becomes Popeye-like. The sudden transformation is comic; the confrontation and interaction with the bully is comoedic—a part of life in prison. Emboldened by the drug, he stares down his cellmate and continues to eat, wrenching a large piece of bread away from his "companion," assaulting him with his food that under "normal" circumstances clearly would have spelled his end, had the guard's whistle not sounded. They rise and begin their march back to their cells, except the Tramp, doped up, who accidentally and inadvertently frees himself temporarily, only to re-enter the jail.

Our attention is always fixed on the Tramp's quick and sudden gestures which undermine, parody and expose the power of his large cellmate established moments before; the prison guards have had their attention fixed on the other fellow prisoner they suspect of smuggling the banned substance. There are actually two scenes within this one scene: the Tramp who dominates his cellmate after ingesting cocaine which we experience as comic and the prison guards' capture of the Tramp's suspected fellow prisoner who had hidden the cocaine in the first place. And just as in the scene with the lost flag that falls into the street during the march, in which the Tramp's identity as a "Communist" leader is clearly misplaced, here, in jail, his role in averting a jailbreak that quickly ensues is nothing short of incidental good luck: he is rewarded with his own private jail cell which transforms his guards into friendly visitors. The door of his cell stays open as he converses with a guard; in his mind, he is there to stay: the model prisoner. And, to add another layer of comedic irony to the scene, the prison authorities are none the wiser to the reality that the Tramp's assumed bravery and quick actions suppressing the jailbreak are the result of his unconscious ingesting of the cocaine in the first place. Playing with the arbitrariness of fortune, luck and chance is part of the structure of the comoedic, making it as absurd as life itself.

The Tramp's walk back to his cell with the others, with its diversion of the jailbreak, is reminiscent of his "ballet" on the factory floor earlier in the film. He captures the perpetrators, disarms them, retrieves their weapon and keys and releases the warden and his staff—he even happily returns the keys.[21] This time, his accidental involvement in a prison riot works to his advantage, or at least one might think. The Tramp is both seen and unseen in accordance with one's preconceptions and points of view. The lorry driver failed to see him, and he is punished; here, the warden sees him and rewards his efforts. Chaplin's point is unambiguous here—the prison class system and its hierarchy is no different than "free" society outside the prison.

The scene's conclusion is carefully juxtaposed against what comes next. The calm inside the prison now shelters the Tramp, "While outside there is trouble with the unemployed." For a brief moment, the Tramp has no trouble being unemployed but willingly adapts to his new circumstances.

The "Trouble outside" scene is by far one of the most disastrous and catastrophic in *Modern Times*. Chaplin guides our eyes as he takes us through these modern times step by step. Scenes are mainly close readings of the intertitle cards—announcement becomes the depiction—and within this self-imposed limitation ("confinement") Chaplin "directs" and constructs. In this scene, which is even less than two minutes long, the labour protest from earlier continues. A wide angle shot shows the economic depression of the "dirty thirties" and its transformation of the street; businesses, as one sign in the immediate background asserts, are "under new management"; the camera angle shifts, and we see the gamine and her sisters scrounge for and salvage broken sticks at the waterfront. Two gun shots from the street intrude on their toil.

The gamin/gamine hands one of the sisters her armful of sticks, and together, they exit the frame; and so does she—running towards and into the street from where she heard gunfire—only to find that her father has been shot and killed. The crowd momentarily disperses as she runs to him but returns as she kneels beside her father with his head in her hands. She is distraught. She has lost everything now that her father has been killed—how Freudian—in a riot in which the Tramp has earlier played an accidental part. How are we to interpret this image? The father's death enhances the looming presence of the other older man, the Tramp. It seals their fate.

The next vignette is a tableaux depicting a family in distress, but from a distance. The emphasis is less on the family's loss than it is on the law taking over—"The law takes charge of the orphans" reads the title card; the three sisters console each other in the shadow of a police officer who stands over them. The two juvenile officers are more concerned about their paperwork on the affair than they are about the newly orphaned sobbing sisters. "Take them away" the title card reads. The two younger sisters are taken away separately (presumably institutionalized), allowing their older sister, the gamin/gamine to escape.

Meanwhile, "Happy in his comfortable cell" "our innocent victim" *languishes* in prison. He is on his back on his bunk (the "bottom" one now), legs crossed, comfortably reading a newspaper. He fidgets with a lock of his hair; he seems almost contented; for a moment, he is back to being himself—naive, self-involved and dreamy. Modern times have improved for him; they haven't for the gamin/gamine.

So, the jail cell, for the Tramp, has become "home sweet home." The scene opens with a direct foreground shot of its interior, where the Tramp has everything he could possibly need or want. Life in prison, as Jeffery Vance describes it, "becomes so pleasant (he is better fed, clothed, and sheltered in the safe and secure prison than in the chaos of society during the Depression)." Here, the Tramp shows unambiguously that he is quite capable of using the system to survive. And we are reminded yet again of the "trouble outside with the unemployed" from the newspaper's masthead which reads in bold uppercase lettering: "STRIKES AND RIOTS!" A sudden close-up shot makes it easier for us to read—it's *The Daily News*—the very present of *Modern Times*: "Breadlines Broken by Unruly Mob." This *textual* and external allusion in the form of a newspaper headline (perhaps one of the most original and effective forms of intertitle card ever conceived) to the previous scene elides the gamine's loss of her father and sisters, since that is not reported on; and the Tramp's lounging in his cell further elides her heartbreak. Thus framed, "modern times" becomes almost a kind of backstory, in keeping with a newspaper trope, and we anticipate the collision of the Tramp's reality with the gamine's.

His cell has all the elements of a comfortable home, right down to the embroidered "Home Sweet Home" wall-hanging—one wonders if he made peace with his previous cellmate who was fond of the craft—along with a portrait of Abraham Lincoln, table alarm clock, painted rocking chair, flower bouquet, flowered bed sheet and fancy pillows. The centred and idolized portrait of Lincoln conjures up the contemporary 1935 film, *The Littlest Rebel* starring Shirley Temple, and Frank McGlynn as the sixteenth president of the United States. It is an image that foregrounds the Tramp's allegiance to the Republic, not his resistance to it. The portrait of Lincoln that hangs in the centre of the back wall of his cell is relevant for what it isn't: a political statement—it is more accurately an aesthetic one. Chaplin here is playing with time as it relates to seeing; the spectators are forced to resist the very movement of film in their effort to focus on the portrait which draws the viewer although it is a static image. His confinement spreads—we are looking in on him; for an instant, the film confines us, forcing our gaze; for an instant, we are inside his cell with the Tramp—the moment we are reading the headlines on the paper he holds, we are there. The portrait punctuates time while representing time—the historical past. It is an aesthetic statement that cannot be separated from its political connotation—it becomes a bad joke about the notion of freedom as opposed to slavery, a freedom which the Tramp gleefully rejects for "the comforts of home" in the face of the portrait—in the face of the "great emancipator." These staged elements engender close reading—they read our reading of film (Figure 1.5).

30 Work

Figure 1.5 Jail cell view of Tramp inside "his comfortable cell" from outside

Summoned from his comfortable cell, he is made to wait with the minister's wife, while both the warden and her husband conduct their affairs out of sight. This is the only scene in the film with any overt religious connotations. (It is a remaining echo of the film's rejected original ending—of the gamine who was to become a nun.) It is an uncomfortable scene in which both their stomachs churn: they are incompatible, although they share this uncomfortable moment. One is reminded of Shklovsky's insight: "Being in the wrong place, not recognizing things—this is the eternal topic of art" (358). Here, both the minister's wife and Tramp recognize only their discomfort. Yet, the scene is also a moment of pause: the spectator is reminded that the film is "comoedic." Here, Chaplin pauses to remind his audience that in comedy, the action exists for the purpose of "imitating characters"; in other words, matters "turn to the ways in which laughter can arise from actions. This can occur," as Simon Critchley, extending Aristotle's poetics in relation to the comoedic points out,

> in various forms: through knowing deception [the "nose powder"], from logical impossibility [the Tramp who continues his nut-tightening

while swallowed by the machine he works "on"], from the possible but entirely inconsequential [the flag scene], from things happening incongruously contrary to expectation [a mime who sings], and from elevated characters becoming base [an uppity or aloof Minister's wife with a bad case of gastritis].

(254)

Moments before, the Tramp was seated next to his large cellmate. The simple juxtaposition of that image with this one is indeed comic.

For his misconceived "role" in foiling the uprising in prison, he is offered parole—freedom—which he promptly declines. "Happy in his comfortable cell," his reason is as comical as it is pathetic—"Can't I stay a little longer? I'm so happy here." The Tramp is uneasy with others and their status. If we are viewing *Modern Times* for the first time, we might openly give the Tramp the benefit of doubt that his next job will finally end in some personal success. Thus far, he has not lived up to his doctor's promise of "avoiding excitement." And the letter of recommendation for employment that the warden bestows on him at the end of this scene might offer him a genuine "second chance." But these assumptions, like those about red flags, are devices intended to construct scenes that will produce the next comic gag. No sooner is he taken on at a shipyard where he collects sticks like we saw the gamine doing with her sisters only a few moments before, than he botches another job by causing a ship that is under construction to become unsecure and slide into the water. As far as second chances go that ship has sailed. He either quits or is let go—we are not told which; "Determined to go back to jail," he exits.

Notes

1. The work of Art in the Age of Mechanical Reproducibility, 1935.
2. Shklovsky and others including Eisenstein, Benjamin and Brecht see Chaplin as an embodiment of their aesthetic: Artistic experience is neither imitation of reality nor the symbolic projection, but an unmasking and a negation in bitter conflict with all those repressive and inhibiting experiences whose nature is never fully known until artistic creation disturbs the surfaces of social, political and aesthetic assent.
3. References to Todd Phillips' film in addition to any others are used mostly to illuminate similarities and differences between *Modern Times* and literally postmodern times—that which comes after "modern times."
4. For purposes of this study, *Modern Times* refers not just to the film but to the times and the aesthetic it—the film and modern times—constructs. Thus, the title carries the "doubleness" of the film: both the troubled historical times and the film in these times.
5. The "Tramp" is literal and that's what he is, and the word is in common currency: meaning tramp, bum, homeless, vagrant, tramping around the streets and

places. "Fleck" means nothing like that. It's meaning in German, for example, is "spot," like soiled spot, or dust spot on your shirt.

6 Chaplin's spelling of the word "gamin" (masculine) as "gamine" (feminine) in *My Autobiography* stands out—he emphasizes its feminine form. We will have more to say about this choice later on.

7 It is difficult to imagine this scene as anything other than a reference by Chaplin to Walter Benjamin's famous 1935 essay, *The Work of Art in the Age of Mechanical Reproducibility*, in which Benjamin argues that mechanically reproduced works of art (like records) are "inauthentic" because the "aura" of their time and place of production, characterized by the unmediated interaction of the artist with the audience, has been commoditized. In this scene, it is almost impossible for the audience not to recall the famous RCA logo and its caption, first introduced in 1900, named after the title of its original painting, "His Master's Voice." Ironically, in the Gospel of John [10:4], Jesus tells his disciples that sheep follow their shepherd "because they recognize his voice."

8 The film shows his polite and civil deference to authority; and the "film" itself shows the effects on him of this deference as the machine also takes on a life of ITS own and fights back at him. The machine has no conscience and just does what it always does: incorporate, digest and assimilate the individual into the machine affectation by affectation until it swallows the worker whole—and the Tramp's whole body. "The more than willing" is, however, a doubleness, because it is part of his deference and civility, which allows the viewer to see and feel the "dissonance" of watching the polite, loyal worker become assimilated into the machine. Moreover, tipping his hat is a doubleness that shows there is something wrong here, something that should be resisted, this should not happen, "our" Tramp should not be going along with this, and laughing at him hurts, because he is so likable and yet THIS happens. So, the "duplicity" is a dissonance in our relationship as spectator to this "enigmatic" person. The "tragedy" ["comedy"] is that the Tramp is trying to be a person but falls into trouble when he tries. Each scene is built on trouble; Chaplin uses doubleness to show it—the mechanical feeding machine; the machine that gorges and then later "spits" back; the fantasy home is countered with the shack, etc. Somehow, despite the darkness in the film, the "person" is rescued by the very woman he himself has tried to seduce. The two of them at the end rescue each other.

9 See also Note 7 (174).

10 The character is described this way in the liner notes to the film (Criterion).

11 The Tramp's rescue by his community of co-workers ends the scene: an inversion of the *King Kong* narrative; indeed, the Tramp of *Modern Times* fits these fluid comic narratives ranging from rampaging monsters to tragic antiheros.

12 In Film Form, Eisenstein argues that

> A dynamic comprehension of things is also basic to the same degree, for a correct understanding of art and of all art-forms. In the realm of art this dialectic principle of dynamics is embodied in CONFLICT as the fundamental principle for the existence of every art-work and every art-form.

13 See Robin Kirkpatrick's "Introduction" to *The Divine Comedy* (Penguin, 2013), p. xv.

14 Meryman 362.

15 "12 Details and References You May Have Missed in *Joker*." (Kirsten Acuna [3 Oct. 2019]. Accessed 7 Apr. 2021).

16 IMDb cites the visible wire that holds the flag in place as a "goof." This one goof especially has aesthetic implications in a film that records and documents many instances of sleight of hand.
17 "Mr. Chaplin's Defense." 23 Sept. 1952. www.theguardian.com
18 Other critics such as Jerry Zaslove might say that "This move was priceless! He is really a good boy. We should like him!" However, there are always consequences, and the Tramp rarely sees let alone perceives them.
19 I am indebted to Karl Siegler for pointing out the structure of this sequence in *Modern Times*.
20 David Robinson commentary on *Modern Times* (Criterion edition).
21 "I thought this move was priceless! He is really a good boy. We should like him!" (Jerry Zaslove, personal correspondence). Meanwhile . . . .

2 Life

Shakespeare said: "All the world's a stage," and Charlie Chaplin said: "All I need to make a comedy is a park, a policeman and a pretty girl" (*My Autobiography* 159).

The Tramp is "determined to go back to jail" well before he meets the gamine—this has been his singular preoccupation all along, beginning with the brief asylum scene; it has been his main concern thus far into the film—"in reality I was a tramp just wanting a little shelter" (146)—and we are almost midway through the film when he finally encounters the gamine in a collision with her (*My Autobiography* 146). The scene takes place at another street corner in an upper-class neighbourhood with high-end pastry shops, a liquor store, "The Globe," parked Ford cars and passers-by in dresses and suits.

She walks out from behind a street corner, "Alone and hungry," pausing to admire the baked goods set-up in the front window display case of a pastry shop. A delivery man carries a tray of breads from his delivery van. A three-word advertisement stencilled across the side of the vehicle foregrounds "home"—"oven to home." The delivery man enters the shop with his tray and the gamine quickly steals a loaf bread from his van—she runs away just as another woman walks out from the corner and sees her. The Tramp who walks out from behind another corner at the other end of the street now faces her—they literally collide. The delivery man returns to his truck and the woman-witness informs him of the theft—points out the gamine's escape—he runs after her, catching her with the Tramp who takes and picks up the bread. The delivery man grabs the "gamine" just when an officer enters the melee. He tells the policeman that she stole the bread. The Tramp intervenes: "No she didn't—I did." For once, he takes action, puts himself in the centre of the occurrence and thwarts the gamine's capture, but not without self-interest, as we shall see. This accidental collision of the two main characters serves to establish the whole second part of the film.

Regardless of his proneness to accidents, it should be noted that the Tramp's comportment always respects social norms and conventions—his

DOI: 10.4324/9780429323317-2

countenance shines a light on their reality and presence in the scene; and as a result, he draws our attention to the physical and class-conscious environment. He plays along and pretends to follow the social rules, but following rules, for him, means accidental breaking of them despite his constant though frustrated attempts at joining *Modern Times* as an active, and privileged and accepted participant-peer—he sees nothing "wrong" about his overriding and more-than-constantly-willing (though hopelessly hapless) desire to "fit in."

In a sense, his encounter—"collision"—with the gamine parallels his earlier encounter with his cellmate. But tables have turned—he, now, is staring down at her. The witness, the delivery man and the policeman all converge on the couple and identify the gamine, not the Tramp as the thief, and they take off in pursuit of the girl. No sooner has the Tramp intruded on the gamine and her plight but he changes course. While left alone outside a cafeteria, he goes in to eat. One comes to see that his fancy dress, his whole comportment and manner is an illusion—a disguise—the joke; it is the way he presents himself that masks his indifference to all around him—which his constant accidents "disclose."

The Tramp's new scheme to "work the system" is to eat as much as he can without paying, while the gamine is pursued off-screen by the crowd of people who have assembled. The Tramp gorges himself—a crime he flaunts when he's done, tapping on the restaurant window on his way out and catching the eye and attention of a police officer who conveniently passes by. The set-up parallels many we have seen that are founded on conventional figure–ground relationships: the primary action in the foreground and the secondary action in the background. This time is no different. Even Chaplin's interior scenes work this way—"Everything ready for the action"— everything built around and anchored to a defining "tableaux." Chaplin makes plain that the Tramp's efforts to get caught parallel the gamine's attempts to run.

He is again in the custody of police by his own plan; the officer takes him by the left hand with his right hand and leads him out; outside of the restaurant, the officer reaches for a police phone attached to the exterior wall to "call it in." The Tramp wastes no time in further securing his arrest by gesturing for a cigar from the clerk of a cigar shop. Replacing his toothpick taken from the counter in the restaurant with a cigar that is lit by the clerk behind the counter in the cigar shop, he starts to smoke with the officer still holding him by his hand. And just to galvanize his base and manipulative intention to get back into his comfortable cell in the jailhouse—undercutting the "genteel" aspect of the Tramp's character—he takes cigars and cigarette packs from the counter and hands the now stolen goods to two young boys who have approached him. He makes the two small children into his accomplices without a thought. The "joke" in this instance is unexpected—we laugh at the social mores the Tramp exploits to his advantage as they reveal the unsaid—his intentions. He succeeds. The officer returns and so does a police patrol car. He is thrown into the "wagon."

Inside the paddy wagon packed with "offenders," bodies clash with bodies; and it is here where the Tramp meets up with the gamine once more. Once again, the scene lasts less than two minutes—but what Chaplin stages is a tableaux of all his former characters from many of his other films that include "immigrants and vagrants and pretty miscreants" (Robinson 458). Chaplin's caricatures have their moments of humanity and vulnerability; here, in the crowded patrol car, they belch and smell, but the Tramp brushes off their "impoliteness"; in fact, this enclosed space, for a moment, illuminates the whole of the social hierarchy. As the Tramp makes his way to his seat, he is framed by "offenders" on each side—at least four of them are formally well dressed wearing hats and ties; two offenders in the foreground are gypsies; he loses his balance and falls on one of the gypsies, a woman of colour who pushes him away with force—the scene recalls his treatment in the jail cell with his oversized cellmate who fancied embroidery and his bottom bunk. No sooner is the Tramp seated than the car stops to pick up the gamine outside a bank, somewhat obscured by a lamp post, which we can plainly see since the set-up inside the car directs our eye from the front where we are situated as spectators to its open back door. This is an intense moment in the vignette, and we know this from the gamine's pensive gaze. She holds the Tramp in that gaze for a moment as he seeks to curry favour with her: "Remember me—and the bread," causing her to turn away in despair—she's street smart and knows what's up. He stands between the "offenders" who are seated next to her and the outside, open space that we catch a glimpse of as the car continues on its way to the police station. More than anything else, the scene in the paddy wagon establishes the essence of the Tramp's true character: he is an ingratiating snob, dressed in the worn-out garb of a Roaring Twenties banker, "keeping up appearances" in a new age of Depression that is also passing him by—he has no place in *Modern Times*. Neither will he ever have any place in the coming post-modern age of the "Talkies," as we shall see when he attempts to speak towards the end of the film, mouthing nothing but gibberish. The comedy of the film is based entirely on this trope—the audience is shown that the Tramp has no place in any age—the comedy is universal—common to all.

It is a moment or scene not unlike the scene in the warden's office where the two characters—the minister's wife and the Tramp—feign politeness, but in this scene in the paddy wagon, the Tramp, when he is shoved inside, is less polite to the male gypsy who belches rudely—the Tramp dismisses him as of the "lower classes." The Tramp makes no effort to ignore the rude behaviour, unlike in the previous scene where he made a much more concerted effort to be polite with someone he considered to be of a "superior class," even reaching for "sound"—the radio—to cover up their churning stomachs. Chaplin enhances our view of the Tramp as shabbily "elegant"—which his (almost) consistently "polite" demeanour parodies. No idealism there. Moreover, if the grandeur of tragedy requires the unity of mind and body, then comedy works through their disunity, where body takes its noisy revenge on the mind. Chaplin's comic plot is structured around laughable events and situations; the characters are buffoonish, ironists or boasters, and the diction is local, common and low (Critchley 254–255). There is no sneezing or belching or farting in *Joker*, for example, a film about a failed comedian. However, *Modern Times*—a dark film about absurd characters and events—is comoedic. Chaplin's composition and direction are subtle: we see that the gamine is picked up and hoisted into the patrol car as it stops in the street adjacent to what appears to be the corner of an imposing "BANK," although one strains to read the letters.

However, unlike the Tramp who wilfully engineered his own arrest, the gamine will not be confined, and she makes a "jailbreak" by rushing the police officer who guards the open back door of the paddy wagon. When it crashes, the gamine, the officer and the Tramp who has followed her are thrown into to the street, which is suddenly empty; the Tramp comes to first and then she does; and then the police officer, whom he quickly knocks out again using the officer's own baton. He urges the gamine to escape and she does, around a corner, but then reappears urging the Tramp to follow her. He pauses—he now has to choose his scheme to get back to jail or go free with her. He goes with her—he chooses her, rather than the comfort of prison system. This is the turning point of the film because the next scene is a fantasy sequence that puts them in their dream home—a middle-class suburban bungalow—together as a couple.

In this sequence, for a moment, the differences between the Tramp and the gamine stand out. She takes for her family—he takes for himself. She is principled; he is unprincipled. She will get him a job—he will lose it. She proves to be more adept at getting along in modern times. Chaplin, too, brings together all the classes in this central scene—the whole strata of the social fabric and changing reality of modern times are brought together as she turns the tables on the Tramp: she seduces him as she coyly smiles while playing with a flower.

The Tramp has tipped his hat in this sequence of collisions, captures and escapes no less than six times. Once more, a notion of politeness, which the camera faithfully and unobtrusively records, is foregrounded. Walter Benjamin sees politeness as an "alert openness to the extreme, the comic, the private and the surprising aspects in a situation" (Symons 135). But the Tramp's polite gestures are similar to Arthur Fleck's laughter: they are not genuine. Each expressive act tends to defamiliarize the scene or situation, punctuating it with something sinister, forthcoming and foreboding—a "concealed" (premeditated) thought. Each works the system—Fleck as we have said, sees through it—and the Tramp, despite his hopelessly hapless efforts to "fit in" is, in the end, worked over the most by it. For Benjamin, as Stéphane Symons points out,

> politeness indicates the ability to not simply *resolve* given conflict but to *extend* it in such a manner that the focus is shifted away from its insurmountably ... politeness makes palpable a way of acting, but only at the instant when all parties are forced to admit their own inability to resolve the conflict.
>
> (Symons 136)

The Tramp putting on his desire to "please" everyone (except the "low-lifes" of the shunned underclass of course, to whom he considers himself to be superior) is very disturbing to the spectator. When we laugh at this it's because we are made to laugh at our own pretentions as well.

Symons argues that Chaplin's camera and gestures dissect "the expressive movements of human beings into a series of minute innervations ... Each single movement he makes is composed of a succession of staccato bits of movements" (143). In other words, Chaplin's "jerky movements" do not simply imitate the assembly line but show the alienating repetition of its experience, which is synchronous with the way the spectator is carried away by "distraction" and habit and thus is integrated into the "machine."

> For Benjamin, Chaplin "could not have made an impact on stage" because this specific type of moving discontinuously inevitably involves the intervention of a machine: the camera "integrates" Chaplin's natural movements to truly re-produce them, that is, to create them anew and thereby modify them into movements that a merely natural body would not normally produce.
>
> (143)

Thus, the spectator's attention is "dissected" by a filmed sequence of recorded images; or, more precisely, by a continuous sequence of discontinuous images, that animate life in the film. For Symons, "the jerky movements of Chaplin's body do not simply *repeat* the movement of the assembly line," for example, "but they mimic it, that is, they share in it, extend it, and thereby *master* it" (143–144). Chaplin's character of the Tramp, however, is not so lucky. There is a semblance of cruelty throughout these scenes—a cruelty that is endemic to Chaplin's and his character's "modern times." Constantly implied in the Tramp's world, it is made completely explicit in Arthur Fleck's post-modern times. The mechanical reproduction of life in a film strip becomes integral to the critique of "modern times." Chaplin comments:

> Cruelty is a basic element in comedy. What appears to be sane is really insane, and if you can make that poignant enough they love it. The audience recognizes it as a farce on life, and they laugh at it in order not to die from it, in order not to weep. It's a question of that mysterious thing called candor coming in. An old man slips on a banana and falls slowly and stumbles and we don't laugh. But if it's done with a pompous well-to-do gentleman who has exaggerated pride, then we laugh. All embarrassing situations are funny, especially if they're treated with humor. With clowns you can expect anything outrageous to happen. But if a man goes into a restaurant, and he thinks he's very smart but he's got a big hole in his pants—if that is treated humorously, it's bound to be funny. Especially if it's done with dignity and pride.[1]

Stéphane Symons, turning to the philosopher Henri Bergson, sees politeness as "agility of thought" (138). From this vantage point, it is clear that the Tramp is also profoundly impolite. "Agility of thought is about the last quality with which one would associate Chaplin's screen-personae," Symons points out, "and in his films a deeply felt affinity for a fellow human being only arises in a romantic context, that is, when it involves a relationship with a single individual" (138). This version of the Tramp's impoliteness—his brashness, even crudeness—is demonstrated when the police patrol car carrying the "offenders" crashes and the Tramp and gamine, along with one other officer, hit the ground and are momentarily knocked out. This is the first time that the Tramp assaults the police, rather than courting them; the second assault occurs, this time once again "accidentally," when he is pushed by an officer for loitering next to a crowd of striking workers and steps on a carelessly placed board, launching a brick. The Tramp's first assault on the cop after the patrol car crashes is nonetheless intentional, which only serves to underscore that he merely pretends "civility"—the classic Comedic "artful dodger" who "gets away with things" and who survives *in spite of* every disaster he is caught up in. The gamine runs away, getting as far as the corner, turns and gestures to the Tramp to follow her. But he pauses momentarily, pensively raising his right hand to his mouth to consider the offer, and just for a second, he stares into the gaze of the spectator. It is a rhetorical move and illustrates his thought behind the action that follows: he decides to follow her—and the audience is tacitly made to understand why by his gaze—and it's not because he cherishes the indomitable freedom she represents. Chaplin reveals the character who "thinks the part"; thus, he balances an action with a thought about the action. "You must be sincere and natural," he asserts, "in order to be convincing" (Ackroyd 90).

The whole sequence that opens with the gamine, "alone and hungry" and ends with the two of them escaping from a chasing patrol car, parallels the earlier sequence when the Tramp is released from the asylum ending up in the middle of a street protest. This time, however, the Tramp is not merely the victim of circumstance but puts himself directly into the centre of the action. He lies to and assaults the police with its own baton no less, after lying about stealing the bread. His taking the blame for the bread incident not a sacrifice, but a ruse to gain the power of obligation over the gamine who is becoming his "love interest," foregrounded by him reminding her of this act when he sees and introduces himself to her in the paddy wagon. The sequence ends with the two of them together—"and hungry." We are here no longer in the realm of blind fate but of active manipulation. Moreover, the Tramp's almost pompous walk illuminates the absurdity of "running away." That is why audiences laugh at his chases.

If we were ever unclear about the Tramp's romantic intentions towards the gamine, we aren't any longer. Her fate is sealed, wedded to his. The score—Chaplin's "Smile" which he composed—reaffirms their fate—and their destiny.

So now, they are both on the run—now they are together—on the road and walking into the foreground where the audience is situated (they will walk away from the audience on a road in the film's final scene). The Tramp points with his cane to a shaded tree on the boulevard at the side of the road in front of a middle-class suburban home. They rest there, surrounded by grass and bushes that seem to have been left to grow wild by the city, and frame the neat lawn of the home which seems out of place in its environment—a small piece of well-kept private property surrounded by civic wilderness. They are a long way from the factory and machines, but we get a glimpse of the encroachment of standardization and sameness of life epitomized by the neat bungalow on the suburban street. The Tramp and gamine have stumbled into another reality—they are socially out of place. Even the sunlight that illuminates this temporary oasis seems bleached and artificial.

The "gamine" changes the Tramp's—and our—perception of her; or, rather, she reinforces a theme that has been building throughout their time together: she makes herself attractive to the Tramp by picking a wild flower from the ground and putting it into her mouth—flirting with him—she seduces him. This shared and pastoral moment feels like a reprieve in the action; and in a profound way, it is precisely that. The Tramp pauses and asks: "Where do you live?" Her answer, "No place—anywhere" prompts him to ponder, conjure and dream. They watch the happy homeowners as they emerge from their house, the wife sending her husband off to work (he wears coveralls under his formal jacket and fedora), she returning with an elated skip in her step to her domestic duties in their home (she wears an apron).

In their mutual "pursuit of happiness," the Tramp and gamine revert to fantasy. For a moment, they step out of "modern time" and reimagine their lives inside this suburban home—at least the Tramp does; we can assume the gamine does as well since she is a willing participant in the fantasy. "Can you imagine us in a little home like that?" the Tramp asks.

The introduction of the title card displaying this question occurs literally at the exact centre of the film—at 43.3 minutes into a film lasting 86.6 minutes in total. Given Chaplin's skill as a director, it cannot possibly have been introduced there by accident.

With this, he also shows himself to be as prescient as he is skilful: largely suburban, American middle-class prosperity peaked in 1971, at which time 61% of Americans comprised the middle class, back down to 49.9% by 2015 (Wikipedia). This year can also be marked as an historical shift from "modern" to "post-modern" times.[2]

Yet, the "suburban home" is disquieting for several reasons. It is a satire of the American dream and thus begins to elide the film's opening premise of "individual enterprise" and "humanity crusading in the pursuit of happiness." Even the homeowners—the couple—seem out of place; their presence foregrounds a role that they agree to play: the factory worker who leaves in the morning; the housewife who gleefully goes about her house work and busyness seeing her worker-husband off. Chaplin speeds up their interaction—something is "unreal" in this scene within a scene: the sped-up movements and gestures of the couple remind us of the assembly line. However, neither the Tramp nor the gamine "imagine" the couple living in the house—both he and the gamine *witness* the couple's actions. And he doesn't mock their happiness—he imitates it before he asks the gamine if she can imagine a life like the one they just witnessed, for themselves.

The following fantasy scene asks us to question the nature of the pursuit of happiness and the jokes—the Tramp who trips over his furniture and clearly does not fit in—even in his own dream; the ease with which he can satisfy his passing consumer craving by reaching for the fresh fruits that grow abundantly just outside the open window and porch; a false or misplaced sense of social status that is simply not earned since everything is already there present for him. The scene is also critical of the dream—of the pursuit of individual and collective happiness—of "paradise," of "utopia," as formed within a mechanized and uncaring society that has lost touch with where and how the products they consume come from. It is a kind of invasion in which the Tramp forces his presence—and the gamine's—on things someone has already created—and on the audience's as well, since this shift in perception directly implicates us when the Tramp, waiting for a cow *to milk itself for him*, stares directly at the spectator: in the fantasy, he and the gamine take everything for granted—there is no work in their lives—only consumption, the agents of which are either ignored or dismissed. This is a world in which *being* has replaced *doing*—a fantasy world in which work has no place in the home.

Their sudden presence in the home which does not belong to them adds a sinister level to the film; moreover, their presence in the "real" married couple's home now underscores their absence, especially that of the housewife who only moments before embraced her husband as she walked with him out of the front door. The Tramp inserts himself into the role of the husband; the gamine, the wife. But the wife is absent in a way that the husband is not—while we observed him leaving for work, in disregarding the wife's work altogether, the scene identifies her role as secondary. The scene shows just how deep the social machinery of the standardization of roles and expectations affects and ultimately erases people in a mechanized modern time—especially housewives. The scene suggests the couple's "real" natures to the audience: two ordinary and desperate people doing whatever they can to fit in while the system hovers over them. They have each other. Maybe. The fantasy home establishes their relationship—they have become wedded.

The whole set-up is ingenious on Chaplin's part because much of the suburban house is hidden from view behind trees and undergrowth that white out some details shot in at a distance under the glare of morning as the two take pause; the undergrowth itself reads almost like a bedding or nest on which the Tramp and the gamine look in on the couple's parting ways, each to begin their own day in their own precisely defined roles within the machinery of modern times and the social world. Only when the woman under the Tramp and gamine's surveillance is entering back into the home are we able to discern some modern conveniences—the floodlights, the small vase of potted flowers on the sill and lone telegraph pole—and recall the smear of speeding cars that pass in the distance behind the gamine, which anticipates the final image of them both on a divided highway. The fantasy shows them buying into the myth of suburban happiness from their nest in the wilderness. It also makes the film's ending more profound since the myth ultimately casts them out; they face the unknown—for themselves and on their own—together; starting over. And in one last iconic gesture he takes their only possessions enfolded in a bundle and throws it over his left shoulder. He carries the past; and the past is seen weighing on them, but its trauma is manageable. The dream home sequence shows them actively reimagining and wishing to rebuild their lives (Figure 2.1 and Figure 2.2).

Figure 2.1 Dream home

Figure 2.2 Dream home (when the cop enters the shot)

From here, we enter into the Tramp's narcissistic fantasy of home life, and it is clearly the Tramp's version of imaginary reality, and not the gamine's. He inserts her into his fantasy. The fantasy is a fragment, but it reveals how they shall live unexamined lives in this suburban home. The Tramp is both polite and impolite: indifferent to anyone else's needs other than his own. In his "ideal" image of the gamine inside "his" dream state, she is reduced to a role—a cog in the social machine—that parallels the reality experienced and embodied by the "real" couple who have already stepped outside in their morning routine of saying goodbye.

The "real couple" is ordinary and stereotyped, but they own a "real home." The "real couple" exit the home together; she stops—calls him back—they embrace; and the man walks away—lunch pail in hand—to work; the woman goes back inside. It is morning. Their "dream home" is thus a metaphor for modern times—foregrounding the utopian myth underlying ownership, gender and socio-economic place. But the Tramp and gamine are out of place; they own nothing; and he isn't working.

Once they are seen inside the home, the darker aspects of the Tramp's world view become most pronounced. The gamine, in a dress and apron—even a bow in her hair—is poised in the entrance way between the living room and kitchen holding a cast iron frying pan which she proudly exhibits. He enters from the foreground and trips over a footstool that is in his way. We expect that, but he pushes the heavier chair away rather than the smaller footstool, a gesture or act we don't expect—he inappropriately removes something other than the very obstacle that tripped him. It is a simple physical gag—we laugh.

But it's rather poignant because it anticipates the final scene when the Tramp and gamine walk away from us on a divided road—what might be the obstacle he fails to see there?

But for now, in the fantasy home, she approaches him, displaying the frying pan. He looks her over, gives her his lunch box (he's presumably returned from his fantasy job for dinner at home with his fantasy "wife"), pats her on the cheek and, without even looking at the pan, places his bowler hat in it. He reveals an open disregard for most objects and things—organic and inorganic—and sees the gamine as merely an object—someone who is there to amuse and serve him. She turns to walk back into the kitchen but if we look closely enough, we notice that she also trips, becoming a little more like him in this imaginary scenario—he sees her as a projection of himself—as if his sameness is spreading, infecting her. He is careless and thoughtless—even here in his fantasy of someone who is as hungry he shows he has no problem with wasting food.

Everything is presented to him; everything is there for his consumption—even the fruit that grows outside his living room window that he reaches for and quickly discards after only taking one bite of it; he even wipes his hands on a curtain as he enters the kitchen. This "impolite" and rude behaviour only scratches the surface—and this from a character who turned his nose up at the deportment of the male gypsy in the police patrol car. The Tramp's "quasi-mechanical manner" here is merely the performance of an unresolvable contradiction: as Stéphane Symons writes, "it works up the attitude to persevere in a stubborn rejection of the status quo" despite his overriding and more-than-constantly-willing (though hopelessly hapless) desire to "fit in" (Symons 139–140). But the scene also says something else: that the excessively polite manners the Tramp displays in public are just that—manners put on for show, to ingratiate himself with others. "Home alone," like in the comfort of his jail cell, he is perfectly happy to take everything and everyone purely for granted.

When the gamine puts the final touches on a large steak she is frying, he readies the table; reaching for an empty pitcher he summons a cow and places the jug under it, which the animal proceeds to fill upon his command. The image of the Tramp summoning this self-milking cow lands somewhere between the comically absurd and the pathetically inept, in that reveals that he does not know how to properly milk a cow—or indeed that they need to be milked at all. In his "idyllic" and imaginary world, living animals like cows are reduced to "automated" feeding (milking) machines.

Nothing in this vignette seems to affect the gamine, who is, like the woman who lives in the house, shown playing a role. The gamine seems to be as compliant and agreeable inside the home in her role as housewife as the Tramp was inside the machine tightening its nuts and bolts—she just as easily adjusts. Waiting for his milk, having summoned the cow to do the job for him, the Tramp reaches for grapes that hang just outside his doorway. Pausing, the camera cuts to the gamine cooking, big bow in her hair, and then shows a close-up shot of the Tramp eating a grape staring at the viewer—another rhetorical move that leaves us feeling as if we have intruded on a scene he controls, flaunts and exploits for his amusement and needs; in this seemingly serene version of "his" reality, its only obvious trope is the Tramp's repeatedly abusive behaviour, in this case especially his terribly dismissive attitude towards animals—expressed most clearly by his kicking the cow that has just milked herself for him, off his porch. Fresh milk—a thick steak—they have it all provided to them. Their table is set and they sit down to eat, vigorously cutting into the steak; their gestures are reminiscent of the "gamin" of the waterfront cutting and stealing bananas. They have everything they could ever want, except none of it is theirs. The image of them both dissolves into a single image of the Tramp, in side-view under the tree in their pastoral setting, pantomiming the steak-cutting and putting pieces in his mouth. The gamine's response, as she drools and massages her stomach with her right hand, is an existential reminder that she is still hungry—that nothing has changed. This gives the Tramp little choice: "I'll do it! We'll get a home, even if I have to work for it." No sooner does he make this declaration than a police officer appears, the gamine alerting the Tramp, lost in a trance of their plight, and they rush away and out of the scene in which they have no place in the eyes of the law.

The Tramp's declaration is comic because his audience recognizes the irony. But he does acquire the chance to "make good" his promise in the next sequence. The officer's sudden appearance at the end of the fantasy sequence is in itself startling, especially since he intrudes in the interstices between the Tramp's waking and day-dreaming life. But his presence is equally a sobering reminder that one is not free from the law he represents: private property. What do the Tramp and gamine do? They run away. The whole scene is a parody and shows how the Tramp exploits and "milks" whatever he can. We recall, however, that exploitation is a characteristic of "modern times." The cruelty of the machine is a trope in the film. The dreamy suburban home is a fake utopia—Chaplin's parody of the American Dream and Henry Ford's America in particular.

Moreover, Comedy—and silent film especially—reveals the unstaged: Chaplin allows us to see something beyond the characters—candid realism:

> It is this realism that is worthwhile striving for—a realism that will portray emotions intelligently and at the same time keep any audience interested in a story. It is a realistic treatment to a point which is true to the times—a modern treatment.
>
> There is a tendency on the screen to overplay emotions. One of the methods used is "registering" them! Often this is accomplished by facial contortions, so badly done that the acting becomes commonplace and unconvincing. I have been striving for simplicity. I have been trying to attain a proper sense of balance.
>
> (*Charlie Chaplin: Interviews* 74)

The situation is often absurd, but its treatment is realistic because that's what makes it comoedic. "I think in make-believe," Chaplin comments, "you have an absurd situation, and you treat it with a complete reality. And the audience knows it, so they're in the spirit. It's so real to them and it's so absurd, it gives them exultation" (Meryman 362).

Even in his dream, the Tramp cannot escape commoditization. And in the next scene, we are thrown back into the realm of consumption—this time into its very temple: the department store.

In the next scene, a department store's night watchman is shown being carried off after breaking his leg, and the Tramp hurries in to apply for the job at the gamine's urging. He is hired after using the formal letter of recommendation that the warden rewarded him with earlier for his "constructive" role in averting a jailbreak; here, similar to moments before, the gamine and the Tramp have everything they could ever want—and need—from food displays to toy displays—however, this is no daydream. In the department store, they need no longer dream of access to consumer goods, they are surrounded by them—but now they remain beyond reach because they can't afford to buy any of them. Here, an even darker reality unfolds and enfolds the "gamine." For now, they cavort around like two kids in a candy store—and they take advantage of the toys—roller skating and playing house. The Tramp is shown his duties, and this part of the film is a reiteration of the first time he is released from the asylum: we follow his eye "consuming" what he sees and beholds—the sandwiches, cakes and wines that are displayed. His gaze lingers, which we track as he stumbles to follow his employer around in this orientation of the store. His longish gaze at these delicacies enacts another inversion of the previous scene in the "fantasy home" when the gamine served him; here, he rushes out for her when the coast is clear once the store is closed for the night and sits her down at a counter and fills her plate—he now serves her, in direct violation of his new job.

The fantasy of consumer bliss from the previous scene is elaborated and concretized once they are left alone in the store. By setting the action in a department store, which was not an uncommon trope of the time—the Marx Brothers did it too—the ongoing critique of Americana is there. The opening scene in the "Toy Department" reminds us that his "love interest" in *Modern Times* is a "gamine"—"a young girl"; here, the "gamine" appears first and foremost a child who reaches first, interestingly, for a toy Mickey Mouse doll—Walt Disney's famous cartoon character created in 1928, and then for a toy metal truck—she "tests" its wheels—a natural reaction borne of excitement, but the gesture also reminds the spectator of the fact that they are watching a film made of parts with images of "real" cars and trucks that crowd the streets in *Modern Times*. They both act like children in their excitement at seeing all the toy dolls, trucks, stuffed animals, coasters, sleds, tricycles and skates; and it is clear as this scene develops that the "night watchman" Tramp sees her in a sexual manner; they are enjoying themselves—they are on a date.[3] It begins with a meal—he takes her to the cafeteria first—and then to the "Toy Department" where they put on roller skates; he puts his on first and skates around her, circling her three times, before skating into the next room where he stops just at the edge of the floor under construction and puts on a blindfold that he takes out of his left coat pocket.

The Tramp's blindfold is itself a sign that he is suddenly self-satisfied—flirting with danger and the gamine—drawing her attention[4]—while at the same time performing a "skill" with virtuosity and accomplishment: the performance is staged, although he puts himself and ultimately the gamine who inevitably rescues him at risk, but he goes even further. His "childishness" seems to endear him to the audience even as it sees the critical double nature of the figure—we ask ourselves why we are not afraid for him, or critical of his risk-taking, and, most significantly, his comic indifference to a clear and present danger. We are meant to fix our gaze on the danger sign which he exploits in this scene. His blindfold forces *us* to see *for him* because we recognize the "danger" clearly visible in the foreground. He does not.

How is one to respond to a clear and present danger? It is "Arthur Fleck" who is a perfect reader of this scene which he experiences in the theatre in *Joker* as he tracks and hunts down its owner, Thomas Wayne. Fleck both laughs with and at the Tramp. In this precise moment, Fleck is transformed into the "Joker"—the "comedian" in him will serve his single-minded and predatory desire now—the unstaged hunter who tracks down Thomas Wayne is now staged in a scene within a scene, staged and unstaged. In his seminal work, *Theory of Film: The Redemption of Physical Reality*, Siegfried Kracauer defines and explores what he calls "staged" and "unstaged" reality:

> I have stressed that films conform to the cinematic approach only if they acknowledge the realistic tendency by concentrating on actual physical existence —"the beauty of moving wind in the trees" as D.W. Griffith expressed it in a 1947 interview in which he voiced his bitterness at contemporary Hollywood and its unawareness of that beauty. In other words, film, notwithstanding its ability to reproduce, indiscriminately, all kinds of visible data, gravitates toward unstaged reality. And this in turn has given rise to two interrelated propositions regarding staging: First, staging is aesthetically legitimate to the extent that it evokes the illusion of actuality. Second, by the same token anything stagy is uncinematic if it passes over the basic properties of the medium.
>
> (60)

Kracauer's observation is insightful as a principle of editing as well, which is integral to the making of films. This scene stands out as "staged" in order for the spectators to see the crucial separation between Chaplin, the masterful director–performer–pantomime, and the smug Tramp character he plays, who once again seems almost "innocent" in the way he enjoys the risk of "playing" in clear and present danger. The comparison between the scene in *Modern Times* and *Joker* illuminates the aesthetic of how the staged and unstaged reality "evokes the illusion of full-fledged actuality" and how "stagey" qualities in a film is "uncinematic" (134). Chaplin seems to know and develop this principle.

In *Joker*, the clip of *Modern Times* is an intrusion, albeit an artificial one, but an intrusion nonetheless that shines a light on and illuminates another historical reality. Furthermore, Fleck experiences *Modern Times* in an ornate theatre during an exclusive fund-raising gala where rich and powerful people are entertained by a character who skates through a temple of consumption, wilfully blind to the danger that awaits him at the margins of his construction site (as it awaits them outside on the street) and not in a popular movie house: stage begets staged. In his essay, "Kracauer's Affinities," Thomas Elsaesser points to Rudolf Arnheim's observation

> for whom the best moment in *Hamlet* is not Shakespeare's text or Olivier's acting, nor even his direction, but a moment when the camera, almost by inadvertence, frames a window of Elsinore castle and lets us see the 'real ocean' in all its force.
> ("Siegfried Kracauer's affinities" np)

The outside real enters the constructed reality of the film in the present. In *Joker*, another reality—another time, the historical past—enters and is incorporated into the present, post-modern film.

The scene in *Joker*, then, points back to *Modern Times*' relationship to post-modern time: we are and were shown how the Tramp is in a clear and present danger; clearly, the Tramp; clearly, the gamine; and clearly, those in attendance at the theatre, especially Thomas Wayne, the object of Fleck's murderous desire, are in a clear and present danger; and, Arthur Fleck himself is in "danger." The Tramp who cannot see because he purposefully hides his eyes with a blindfold is in a clear and present danger to impress the gamine—"Look! I can do it blindfolded!"—causing her to rescue him, putting her in "clear and present danger"—in solidarity with him—as well. The Chaplin of *Modern Times* could not know of or envision this interaction between the two films; Todd Phillips' film extends and illuminates the danger of "modern times" that was always "clear and present" to Chaplin in his day; but now, it is seen from the objective vantage point of the post-modern Fleck *cum* Joker. Fleck and both audiences watching both the films are simultaneously in clear and unclear—unseen and unnoticed—danger.

Blindfolded, there is no danger: for the Tramp, if you don't see it, it doesn't exist; in understanding that meaning of the blindfold, Fleck becomes the greater threat because he sees through the myth of modern times. The sign that warns of danger in *Modern Times* is unambiguous; it is construction site-specific—a physical and visible sign that is placed next to danger—the section of floor that is under construction and temporarily without a barrier or balustrade, but it is also site-specific in relation to the film as a whole, since it points back to the lost flag scene in the film and its multiple meanings that are dependent upon "ways of seeing," from the standpoints of both the characters and the spectators. There is no ambiguity here; however, danger is as danger does. Moreover, the danger Fleck—the "hunter"—embodies is projective—it is obsessed with Thomas Wayne, the "hunted." The Tramp ignores the danger sign placed in the foreground of the tense scene in *Modern Times*, but there is also danger in the gamine's rescue of the Tramp when she takes his blindfold off him. The scene recalls the danger and confusion that the "red" flag created in the street earlier. And just as the flag scene situates the spectator in the immediate foreground of the dangerous action, the scene in *Joker* similarly places the spectator with the audience who are looking down on the original scene in the film *Modern Times*. The audience in the Wayne Theatre, unaware of the disguised Fleck, experiences *Modern Times*; however, the contemporary spectator experiences not only Fleck's deception in the film *Joker*—separate from the audience in the Wayne Theatre—but also the scene in *Modern Times*—*together with* the audience in *Joker*. We participate in their laughter at the scene; or, at the very least, we "see" them; "they" do not know we are there. The film that they are watching—*Modern Times*—is their blindfold in relation to "us" watching the Arthur Fleck character become "Joker."

The scene in the theatre showing Chaplin's film is set up by the scene that takes place outside of the theatre. Fleck barges into a crowd of demonstrators that has gathered on the street. In *Modern Times*, we have seen that the Tramp is usually breaking away from crowds one way or another; however, in *Joker*, Fleck observes the laughter of the crowd. He's detached from them at this point and then begins mimicking their laughter and their protest gestures. It is a chilling apprenticeship to a mob that he will embody and transcend in the form of a "super hero." Once inside the theatre, Fleck disguises himself as an usher—the camera stays on him as he cautiously ascends the elaborate, opulent vaulted stairway that leads to the theatre's main entrance, which he quietly enters. He is now in the centre of the screen. He takes a couple of slow steps forward holding onto the gold banister that divides the open walkway and stands at the balcony's edge looking down; he is still in the centre, but he shares it with the Tramp who continues roller skating blindfolded in the film *Modern Times* that is projected on the screen. Fleck's gleeful expression seems to indulge the Tramp, who courts disaster. The danger is both immanent and entertainment. We see in this double image—this parallel scene—two characters at the edge—both are in imminent danger and both *are* the danger: the Tramp who acts out his indifference to danger by wilfully blinding himself to it, and Arthur Fleck who once again mimics characters including the Tramp of "modern times" in addition to his idol, Murray Franklin (played by Robert De Niro), a "veteran talk show personality" and host of "Live with Murray Franklin."⁵ For a moment, Fleck appears to inhabit the talk show host, "hosting" the Tramp. His gestures in this scene anticipate his "live" encounter with Franklin later in the film. The scene renders Fleck emotionally vulnerable—underneath, he wants his idol to adore him, but there is also "music in Arthur—like Chaplin—a quiet grace and elegance"⁶ that is visible to the viewer. However, in this same moment, Fleck is human again—his laughter this time is synchronous with the audience's—it's almost natural. He reawakens as "Joker" the moment he sees his nemesis, Thomas Wayne, in a VIP section of the theatre. The Tramp is incapable of Fleck's internalized emotional depth because he refuses to accept the role his society has created for him—he can only put himself in physical, not psychological, danger (Figure 2.3 and Figure 2.4).

The set-up of the two scenes in *Joker* is significant and reveals the threat in both scenes; and, both scenes break the walls of theatrical illusion. The Tramp transforms the department store into a theatre full of "spectacles" for "childish" amusement—the toys and his performance on skates; and Fleck brings the ethos of the street—the rage of the mob which he, thus far has shared, but is still able to suppress—into the baroque Wayne Theatre. In *Modern Times*, the spectator watching the scene is rendered mute, situated safely behind the sign announcing the "danger." In *Joker*, spectators are seated "above" the image on screen and Fleck is in the centre aisle walking in and so an emotional fall is not only an imminent danger for him, but danger is immanent throughout the scenes. This nuanced gesture when Fleck makes an entrance is significant—we are given power over the Chaplin

Figure 2.3 Roller skating (scene from *Joker*)

Figure 2.4 Fleck watches Chaplin (scene from *Joker*)

image, but not in relation to Fleck, who is unbalanced by his metamorphosis from pseudo-usher to a psychotic killer.

Thus, films beget films—films assimilate other films and construct their own histories. The antecedent *Modern Times* intrudes on the post-modern *Joker*. Their inclusion is intentional and staged as a film within film. The staged presentation of *Modern Times* "inside" the film *Joker* presents the audience with a whole other universe, an unstaged surplus reality that reveals another dimension, another time; albeit, by now an "ancient" one. From the vantage point of the post-modern, audiences experience both scenes in *Joker* and *Modern Times* simultaneously—moreover, the juxtaposition is intentionally disembodying. For a moment, we inhabit the interstices between the staged and unstaged reality by the director using both films to momentarily place us outside of history—to create a "post-modern time"; yet, we are united in our separate experiences: Fleck, who watches *Modern Times*, watches the audience watch *Modern Times*; the spectator-audience of *Joker* watches Arthur Fleck watching *Modern Times* watching spectators in the theatre watching *Modern Times*; each of these entities are separated by time, space (place) and class from the images projected on the screen in the Wayne Theatre. The parallel scenes reveal a latent object or detail that otherwise would go unnoticed, and this is what the "film" captures in the theatre when Fleck interrupts *Modern Times* with both probing and sinister motives; when he "connects" with the film, those motives are suspended temporarily. In *Modern Times*, that "unnoticed detail" is the predatory nature of the Tramp character. "Chance meetings, strange overlappings and fabulous coincidences" reveal and illuminate the unstaged (Kracauer 19). The scene in *Joker* that includes a scene from *Modern Times* is an extension of this principle of "unstaged reality." The aesthetic principle of "unstaged reality," then, "chance meetings" and "fabulous coincidences," in this case—the clip from Chaplin's *Modern Times*—establishes Arthur Fleck's epiphany: the pivotal moment when, as an usher in disguise, he observes the Tramp of *Modern Times* roller skating wilfully blind to his "real" situation. In this moment, Fleck makes himself wilfully blind to *his* "real" situation as a failed comedian and learns that he can carry on as a "Joker": a psychotic killer. This poser—this staged usher in disguise—introduces a new epoch, but for now, it remains unstaged: it is as yet a premonition of evil. Once again, this scene within a scene allows us to see (something—a danger) beyond the characters.

In a way, the roller skating sequence is also a consistent extension of the former sequence that included the Tramp's "life fantasy" with the gamine. He goes out of his way not to see what he doesn't want to see. It is clear that the Tramp doesn't care about where and how the food and the comforts of home are created and nurtured by the products of the labour of others. The former scene imagines an impossible reality; and this scene expresses, once again, his almost brutal and cold indifference to life—he blinds himself to all things inconvenient, only to have to be "rescued" by his gamine from a danger that he puts himself into with his blatant disregard of the warning sign. He stumbles when the gamine rescues him from danger—and without his blindfold, the Tramp must once again "see" reality, but he can't.

Once he has been validated by the gamine's rescue, he then proceeds with "putting her to bed." Chaplin situates the Tramp languishing on a love seat smoking a cigar—he is there to be entertained. The gamine complies as she parades in her white bathrobe between him and a display bed. Suddenly, the Tramp is insistent. He "skates" over to her, "disrobes" her and commands her to bed. The scene conveys a clear image of child abuse by a father figure. She gets into it and he covers her with the bathrobe. The sequence is so unsettling and unnerving, one cannot help but see it. We are not doing this. But we are certainly seeing what Chaplin shows—the darker, seamy underside of life as the characters are experiencing it in this scene.

The scene's most disturbing image is of the Tramp putting the gamine to bed on the "Fifth Floor. Bedroom Display." She wears a white fur coat or bathrobe.[7] The dirty smudges on her face are gone—she's been cleaned up. This would fit the image of the bathrobe; she is ready for bed. David Robinson argues that the fur coat transforms the gamine, a destitute orphan, into the film star "Paulette Goddard." But it also transforms her "class" and makes her "like" the Tramp whose "costume" or wardrobe represents the business "classes" of the "Roaring Twenties." If one reads the scene in this light, then Chaplin is pointing out their off-screen relationship. On screen, the image is disturbing and conjures up something darker. Robinson uses the word "touching" in his commentary to describe her delight in the toy department, and he points out that "the first toy she picks up is the Mickey Mouse doll." In this sequence, Chaplin presents the contradiction: she is a child attracted to toys; a "movie star" transformed by a white bathrobe; a gamine—"a small, slim, pert young girl"—the Tramp "puts to bed." Consider the "set-up": she shows off her white bathrobe opening and closing it (dressing and undressing) for him (in front of him) while he lounges smoking a cigar taking her in. The child-molesting aspects of his desire for the gamine when he "puts her to bed" in the department store cannot go unnoticed or unacknowledged, especially since he juxtaposes this "crime" with another—the burglary which he yet again inadvertently (while drunk and still on roller-skates) defuses—especially when we consider its "set-up."

Here, Chaplin's comoedic cruelty is candidly fully expressed and shown. He makes the gamine into an object for his entertainment and pleasure—an object of his desire. He commodifies her in a department store, no less, in "bedroom displays." He puts her on display. In this predacious scene, the Tramp's cigar, which he was passing out to minors before, is both a joke that recalls jokes, but it is also not a joke—it is a revelation of character since it points to his innate

Figure 2.5 Ellen models her robe/coat

Figure 2.6 "Bedroom display"

desire for the gamine. But it is neither funny nor comic. If *Modern Times* is a dark film—and it is—then it just got considerable darker. This is not a case where "sometimes a cigar is just a cigar" (Figure 2.5 and Figure 2.6).

Three burglars scatter when they hear the Tramp exit the elevator on his rounds; he continues to skate "punching the time clocks" and is soon ambushed by two of them; he is shot at as he tries to climb a working escalator (still on roller skates). The moving escalator delivers the Tramp to the burglar who props him up in front of barrels of "choice old rum and sherry wine" and he is searched. The Tramp stumbles and startles the burglar who again shoots at him but misses, hitting the barrels of rum and wine which begin to discharge. The Tramp, regaining his composure, is sprayed by the discharging alcohol which quickly inebriates him. The scene is juxtaposed with an image of the gamine asleep in bed. The action picks up again with the three burglars intending to restrain the Tramp with rope but "Big Bill," one of the burglars and the Tramp's former co-worker, recognizes him. They embrace and share a drink; establishing solidarity with the thieves. Once again, the Tramp, while under the influence, foils a robbery inadvertently. The scene becomes a comic inversion of the jailbreak sequence—this time, the Tramp is on the side of the criminals. But like the gamine, they are acting without criminal intent—"We ain't burglars—we're hungry" says the title card, establishing a class-based solidarity between the unemployed, the Tramp and the gamine.

"The next morning," *not having had to rely on the Tramp's assurance that he would wake her up in time when he put her to bed*, the gamine wakes up early on her own and manages to escape the department store before it opens. The Tramp, on the other hand, who has "slept in" drunk, is awakened in "Women's Apparel" under a mound of fabrics. The scene recalls the one in the street where he found a flag. To him, an "innocent bystander," it meant nothing other than a lost object. Here, the fabrics—on sale in "Women's Apparel" in a department store—have obvious monetary value. Even the shirt off his back is perceived by an unknowing female patron to be of high quality, since her reaching for it shows her interest in its value, inadvertently uncovering the Tramp who ostentatiously wears it—he is "dis-covered" by this older woman who examines an interesting fabric that turns out to be the Tramp's original clothing. Meanwhile, it is business as usual for the store and its consumers go about their shopping as the Tramp is arrested and taken to jail for (presumably) dereliction and abuse of his duties—good for him—once again allowing the State to take care of him. The look of anguish on the gamine's face as she waits for him outside the store (it's been over three hours since her own escape) and recalls her heartbreak at the sight of her father lying dead in the street. The Tramp gestures her away, presumable for her own good—so she won't be implicated in the misdemeanours—and she is back on the street. He gets to go back to jail. The Tramp's fantasies have almost come true, only to wreck him once again.

"Ten days later" and the gamine is waiting for him on his release from jail—but this time she belies her role as a gamine. Chaplin clearly shows her prominently jutting out her womanly breasts as she leans backwards against the building. The gesture is unmistakable. The following two montage sequences are direct parallels to and analogous with two earlier episodes that include the opening scene in the factory and the Tramp's fantasy vignette with his love interest the gamine. Their walk away from the police station down the street is another good illustration of the polite-impolite Tramp. We see him change his position as they walk away together—he takes the conventionally proper place beside her on the unprotected side which places her on his right; as he manoeuvres this change of position he comes up against a lamp post and nearly crashes. His response to this inanimate object becomes machine-like: "a mechanical and non-differentiating repetition." He tips his hat to it (Symons 139).

This time, however, the sequence is told more fully from the gamine's vantage point—she is, after all, the one who finds them a home—her

Life 57

"authority" alongside the Tramp's is more overt in this scene—she is taking charge while at the same time falling into the role of the stereotypical housewife.

She is now completely fulfilling her role as the Tramp's love interest; she has been dutifully waiting for him while the Tramp is incarcerated for "ten days." "I've got a surprise for you. I've found a home," she exclaims when he is released and they embrace. Chaplin poses them both in front of a "dilapidated shanty shack, a comic version of the Hoovervilles" and shanty towns "of the period" cobbled together on the bank of a dirty industrial park, as a couple (Vance 215). They stand, face to face with its reality, their backs to the audience.[8] The ramshackle home resembles a cartoon, but at least they stand together on an equal footing with one another facing it, unlike the previous fantasy home scenario in which they sat on the ground on the side of the road outside of the scene within a scene, looking in and dreaming (Figure 2.7 and Figure 2.8). For a moment, there is little humour in the scene; this is a familiar environment for the "gamin"; we are back on the waterfront. And since their backs are shown towards us, we do not know what they are thinking. Suddenly, her naïveté reveals itself in her exuberance for the shack, despite its condition and the Tramp's lingering apprehensions which border on a

Figure 2.7 The ramshackle home

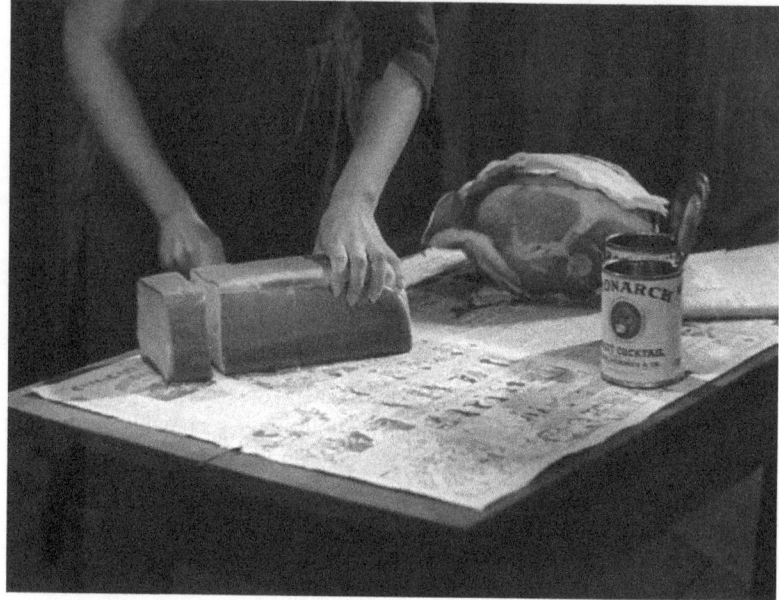

Figure 2.8 Breakfast table with comics

casual indifference. Their new "reality" parallels, nonetheless, the fantasy life from before—the gamine is hopeful. She exudes the pride of being a homeowner in this scene and goes about making repairs and preparing meals while the Tramp is attacked by the home. However, the only reality that creeps into that former fantasy is memory of hunger. An intertitle card makes the ironic point: "It's paradise," exclaims the Tramp, but no sooner is he standing motionless over the threshold under the doorway than a board above him falls and hits him on his head; it would seem that the house itself rebukes first impressions. A potted bouquet of healthy flowers rests on a makeshift table in the centre of the ramshackle room that recalls the smaller pot of flowers that sat just outside the idealized version of their fantasy suburban home. It is a leftover; an uncanny reminder of the same object in the earlier scene of the idealized home.

The fantasy home has marked an important touchstone in the narrative and also a foreshadowing of how the film must end with the characters' emerging realities of life and work. Scenes that follow throw them back into the machinery of labour and social pressures. The ramshackle home reinforces a dominant theme throughout: abandonment. Moreover, this new home is important for what it is not: "Of course it's no Buckingham

Palace." The gamine's ironic comment shines a light on the reality of what it is: an abandoned shack adjacent to a dismal industrial park. She is the one who finds it and recalls our first introduction to her as a "gamin": "a child of the waterfront." And it is at this point in *Modern Times* that the film takes on a grimier look: discarded empty tins serve as drinking cups; things fall apart and the wall, the floor, the board that falls and hits the Tramp on his head as he enters, is a reiteration of the classic silent film running gag of being hit on the head with an object—an event that is similar to the scene earlier in the film when the police patrol car crashes and the Tramp knocks out a cop with the cop's own baton just as he is coming to; the gag also anticipates the scene outside of the factory when the Tramp inadvertently hits another cop with a brick. Every situation is a transition into another situation or some other scene within the scene that remembers and references other scenes outside of it and builds upon them; each scene is as much a characteristic as the characters are themselves. The characters cannot be separated from the scene—they can only recall or foreshadow other scenes. Here, the decrepit shack recalls an earlier version—albeit a fantasy—of "home." They are mirror opposites. In the fantasy home, the Tramp and gamine are the intruders, and the Tramp abuses the home, but this shack is falling apart and nearly falls in on the Tramp. Thus, the "rot" and decay in the dilapidated shack is already there—the Tramp merely disturbs it and brings it to life. And what are the consequences this time? He is made to sleep in what appears to be a woodshed or a doghouse. The image takes us back to his "comfortable cell" and his satisfied compliance with living in one. Here, he sleeps soundly, turning to his advantage whatever storm that follows.

The jokes and gags that centre on the shack draw our attention to this new world of the ramshackle. The Tramp in the fantasy from previous scenes abused the home; here, the shack abuses the Tramp. The roof falls on his head; he falls through the wall and the floor. The shack is surrounded by a barren wasteland. The factory in the distance, on the horizon, functions almost like a mirage.

The gamine fixes the fallen board and secures it in place; in this gesture, this analogue scene to the fantasy home reverses the characters' roles. The Tramp assumes a more passive place in her paradise on the bank of a muddy industrial park. He gets out of her way, leans on her table and it crashes, smashing the pot of flowers. She removes the table, and he reaches for a broom that holds up a side of the wall of their shack, and it crashes. She comes to his rescue once again and restores the wall using the broom to prop it back up in place. Next, he leans up against the opposite wall and falls through into the pool that is next to the shack. Then, it is night: she sleeps inside the shack next to the table which has been restored; he is asleep in a woodshed/doghouse attached to the shack. The image of the Tramp asleep in his "pen" reminds audiences that he likes tight spaces. He is comfortable in confinement. Chaplin emphasizes this penchant for confinement by using a direct foreground shot to show the shack and the smaller shanty attached to it, which then dissolves to an interior shot that shows the Tramp soundly asleep; a third shot in the sequence shows the shanty again in a full shot which then dissolves into another foreground shot that pans down from a bird's eye view of the gamine asleep on the floor in the centre of the house. The shanty shack is a metaphor for their relationship which intensifies since Chaplin takes the time to show them both asleep—an intimate moment. She is given a privileged space while the Tramp takes the doghouse. They have come this far and now "share" a home.

In *Modern Times*, no one is seen favourably, especially not women who are presented as domestics and/or foils for entertainment, epitomized by the café owner near the end of the film who sees a marketing opportunity in having the gamine dance for his establishment in the street. The men have their protest riots and marches; a semblance of change for better or worse is always in the air, but the women, with the eventual exception of the gamine, are fixed in their limited roles. They are cooks, cleaners, secretaries, objects to be pursued—entertainment—even "tattletales." And, in the original ending, even "aloof" as nuns. Men are employees and employers—presidents and foremen; women sit on the sidelines, like the minister's wife who uncomfortably waits with the Tramp earlier in the warden's office.

Chaplin shows us another image of the ramshackle home which recalls the earlier dream scene. It is indeed presented in stark contrast to its earlier fantasy version. The Tramp emerges under the new light of day, gleefully exiting his little shanty to take a swim in the basin nearby. He reaches the end of the dock, readies himself and then dives into the water. But he never tests its depth first (which would be a natural thing to do upon entering an unknown body of water, especially one in an abandoned and vacant industrial park). He is carried away by superficial routine, oblivious to the water's shallow bed, though he learns his lesson and exits the basin with a sore head. Even the natural environment seems to want to remind him that he is out of place, out of his depth. He stumbles back and enters his shanty.

Chaplin juxtaposes this scene with an interior close-up shot of a piece of meat frying in a pan and the gamine cutting thick pieces of bread on her table. Everything about these details is overloaded; however, one wonders where all the food has come from since this is no dream. The Tramp exits his "pen" and knocks "politely" on her door, wiping his feet ("politely"); and he enters and bows to her (politely). His gestures of politeness in this sequence ironically remind us that this is "no Buckingham palace"; they go about their busyness in ways that reiterate the earlier vignette in the suburban home. Moreover, as he bows to her, we catch a glimpse of the wasteland outside that is filmed in a diffusing shot that resembles a dust storm. He slams the door shut and is knocked out again, though he and his audience expected that. The accident with the board foreshadows the accidents that will ensue in the next factory episode.

The gamine proves to be a good apprentice of the Tramp's. He takes note of her carefully set table, on top of which she has placed a newspaper open to the comics. She's becoming more fully a person since the last time we "read" the funnies in this film was in the president's office in the opening scene; here, she puts the newspaper to use and makes something more out of it: a table cloth. He takes notice of a large piece of smoked ham, picks it up and playfully inquires as to *how* she got it; she takes it from him and winks—she's bringing home the bacon now, and it's by illicit means. In the profoundest sense, she has become, like the "automated" milking cow in the former fantasy scene, a provider with her own resources. They both sit, but again their position at the table parallels the scene in the fantasy home with one nuanced exception: she sits on the left-hand side of the screen; he, the right-hand side—their seating is reversed in alignment with their power structure in the shack, which is hers. As soon as he sits down his chair falls through the broken floorboards. Remnants of the former dream outlast the reality being lived in her shack; as she moves the table by herself to a new location the spectator can see another bouquet of potted flowers on the window sill which diffuses into white and grey. They each take bites of their sandwiches that are so big they have to separate the halves in order to manage them. A change in modern times is announced on the front page of a newspaper that the Tramp picks up off the table—it is *The Daily News*—the name brings us back to his former comfortable life in jail when he had time for reading headlines: "Prosperity Has Turned the Corner" they read. "Factories Reopen! Men to Be Put To Work."

"Work at last," he gestures: "Now we'll get a *real* home," he exclaims with exuberance (emphasis added). If the fantasy home wasn't real and this one isn't either and cannot be sustained by their situation, then what is reality? The ramshackle home, a parody of the ideal suburban dream home, is like most cartoons, reductive. Reality slips between the two images of home, with the Tramp stumbling back and forth: the situations that the scenes are built upon are real. The Tramp, where he uses the word "real," conjoins and links the two scenes: the suburban home becomes a version of reality in the sense that it belongs to another real couple—their reality is reaffirmed by the Tramp and gamine's witness of them, in addition to the spectator's observation of them, even though they are imitated by the Tramp. The gamine's home is real; her view of the shack is closer to reality because she recognizes that it is the other side of the Tramp's daydream.

The neglected shack is closer to their reality as they experience it: each has been abandoned.

One other detail stands out in the scenes of the ramshackle home, and we have already touched on it. Dilapidated and in shambles, it seems to mock the Tramp, especially while the gamine proves that she can function in it "normally." She does the repairs and cooks. The shanty shack's rebuke of the Tramp shines a light back on his parody of the fantasy home and its couple: his parody was aimed at the life inside of the home and not the home itself, which he takes full advantage of in his dream. But here, now, this ramshackle home becomes a parody of the Tramp in the manner in which it falls apart.

Though "Work at last" might be wishful thinking, off the Tramp goes running back to the beginning: factory life. He rushes out and the gamine follows and stops just outside her doorway mimicking the same gestures the woman made in the former episode in the "suburbs." Roles have set in and they are more a part of the mechanized "modern times" than the couple realize, and their actions, especially the Tramp's, belie. He is determined by the machinery and can operate none of it. We "expect" at this point an antagonistic relationship—a summing up.

The Tramp gets his way—he rushes through a crowd—the one crowd that he bullies his way through, and one hire as the last man who pushes his way through the crowd to get through the gates before they close. And this time his employment isn't terminated by being fired—his co-workers go on strike. He does not willingly participate in the strike, yet he becomes an instigator inadvertently, the catalyst for another riot. In fact, the "crowd" becomes a character, an amorphous lethal figure, which *Modern Times* animates as a force; moreover, fear is always around the corner.

For the time being, however, he is a "mechanic's assistant." We see him stumble (again) with his oversized and loaded tool box, but he is ill-equipped to handle his new "role," nearly causing serious physical harm to his associate by destroying an oilcan which is flattened by the machine. The Tramp is unvexed by this and suggests a new use for the crushed oilcan as a small shovel, which he mimics for his employer with digging gestures. The "semantic shift" from oilcan to shovel does not impress his colleague and boss. History repeats itself but worse, and once again, the Tramp is responsible for destroying his associate's pocket-watch—a "family heirloom"—which he had left in his coat pocket. The machine flattens and destroys it.

It this seemingly innocuous scene, Chaplin exploits the conventional prop-gag through a random act of destruction; and yet, that is precisely why it stands out—it is a destructive act illuminating a constructive idea of family and companionship. The destruction of the pocket watch—"a family heirloom"—recasts the characters in the scene as fully and specifically human. The Tramp's second factory job, this time as a mechanic's assistant, is different in kind from his earlier experience in the factory as an assembly line worker. He has a title—"assistant." Now he assists a mechanic, becoming fully machine-like himself in the sequence when his mechanic is gorged by the machine. The event and confusion recall the opening sequence in the factory when the Tramp was swallowed whole by the machine, but this time it cannot be made to reverse and run backwards. We recall that he merely kept repeating the gestures of work in the former scene, unaware of what was happening to him. But here, his co-worker is fully aware of his plight; and when lunch comes, the Tramp force-feeds his master who has become stuck in the machine. The Tramp returns the violence to his new co-worker that was done to him by his former Capitalist-factory owner boss in the earlier sequence featuring the mechanized feeding machine. But before we get to the moment in this second factory scene when the Tramp transforms himself into that feeding machine, there is a scene in which the mechanic is checking gauges and looks away while his family heirloom is destroyed. The mechanic's exclamation of loss comes as a jolt, reminding us of what the gamine has lost, as well—her sisters were taken by the juvenile authorities and her father was killed in a riot on the street. In *Modern Times*, we see character types enacting their roles—part of the rank and file—either escaping the system or being part of the system. But when they become "people," it is unnerving. From this destructive act of flattening the mechanic's watch an idea surfaces that the final, closing image of the Tramp and gamine foregrounds and reinforces: they have become a family of sorts; or, at the very least, their future points in that direction.

The structure of the scene revolves around the word "idle" in the title card that establishes context: "The mechanic and his new assistant put to work repairing the long idle machinery." Of course the audience knows by now that in the context of *Modern Times*, "idle" is synonymous with "unproductive," "wasteful" and "unprofitable." The huge machine made of turning gears and parts of all sizes is now no longer idle and dwarfs both the mechanic and the Tramp. Everything is oversized, right down to the long, extended oilcans and tool box which the Tramp can hardly hoist—and as he attempts to strap it to his back it spins him around and he lands on the floor next to the machine. The Tramp's out of control bumbling around with and clumsy handling of the awkward toolbox contrasts the orderly movement of the machine and all its spinning parts. The mechanic is not amused. His frustration anticipates the angry patron in the restaurant scene near then end of the film. The mechanic's careful studying of the blueprints he carries, several of which are rolled up in his jacket and trouser pockets, anticipates the final scene that involves the Tramp practising his song and dance routine, aided with the lyrics the gamine writes for him on his shirt cuff. Both are working off a script for the purpose of the joke which involves both of them being unaware of what the other is actually doing. The Tramp replaces the destroyed oilcan with a new one; the mechanic checks his pocket watch, puts it back in his jacket, and the Tramp puts the jacket on the machine next to the second oilcan. We can anticipate what follows: the Tramp saves the second oilcan, but not the jacket with the valued pocket watch.

The scene also makes the point of juxtaposing the Tramp and mechanic with the Leviathan-like machine that gorged the Tramp's master. The Tramp mimics the countenance and comportment of his master just as another worker enters the scene to inform them both that the factory is on strike—again. If they were not "equals" before in work, they are now—this time their job has been "flattened" and the machine is sidelined—"idle"—once more. In their final pose together, Chaplin unites them—one notices almost a family resemblance in their appearance.

The machinery in this sequence is far more imposing, and "heavier," than before. It is also dirtier. It seems ready to "fight back," which it in effect does by swallowing the mechanic, then resisting any and all attempts to make it work efficiently again. They are both on top of it—the mechanic is testing levers and gears; the Tramp stands by with his large tool box that he is told to remove. He repositions the toolbox and the mechanic starts up the machinery. The toolbox falls into its gears and is destroyed; the machine spits out the metal tools, reanimated, almost in defiance of the Tramp who adopts boxing poses in an effort to defend himself from its workings.

Not only does the last sequence in the factory parallel the scene at the beginning of *Modern Times*, it reminds the spectator of the violence of industrialization; moreover, it depicts an internalized violence which the Tramp now unleashes on his colleague. His associate gets "caught up in the cog wheels of a gigantic machine of doubtful purpose," and as it did for the Tramp in the opening sequence, swallows him; however, when "he becomes completely stuck," and as David Robinson points out, "Charlie considerately feeds lunch to his protruding head" (*Chaplin: His Life and Art* 467). But Robinson is mistaken about this: the scene has nothing to do with "consideration." He may look considerate towards his colleague to Robinson and the audience familiar with his "politeness," but in reality, the Tramp becomes as dispassionately ferocious as the mechanized and automated feeding machine that fed him earlier—he has internalized it. The Tramp is utterly lost within the machinery of "modern times," as indicated by his head-scratching gesture at the start of the scene—he simply does not "know." However, the Tramp's actions feeding his distressed colleague are played indifferently mechanically: the scene reminds us of the violence and abuse the Tramp himself has suffered and internalized. Unlike that earlier sequence, however, the mechanic is fully aware of his distress. He is fully cognizant of the fact that he is where he should not be. In the earlier sequence, the Tramp who was gorged by the machine merely continued "working." Now, the tables have turned. When the lunch bell sounds the Tramp breaks, fetches his lunch, sits down and begins eating. His associate, still inside the machine, asks for his lunch and the Tramp brings him his lunch box. What ensues is on one level, the Tramp abiding by his associate's instruction to retrieve his lunch; on another level, we observe the full transformation of the Tramp into a machine commensurate with the mechanical feeding machine from the earlier scene in *Modern Times*. *Modern Times* has finally caught up with the Tramp. He performs the "role" of worker in modern times superficially, automatically, destroying faith in work, while almost destroying his colleague (Figure 2.9).

Over the course of the film, the narrative advances from accident to accident; from one troubled situation to the next, with the Tramp and gamine just one step ahead. *Modern Times* follows them everywhere and pervades even their dreams—they seek refuge in their time by conforming to it. It pursues them as much as they pursue it. And in this second, and last, factory scene, we come full circle: the Tramp becomes the machine which feeds and gorges. The force with which he feeds his confined colleague parallels the ferocity of the mechanical feeding machine. In this scene, it

Figure 2.9 The Tramp as feeding machine

is the Tramp who finally gets to eat, not the mechanic. He unleashes every hardship that he has within him on his fellow co-worker who suffers. The scene is unsettling because it shifts our attention back to where the violence now resides: internalized in the Tramp. He shows that he is capable of such forceful indifference. The Tramp never gets depressed; rather, he becomes violent—as violent as *Modern Times*. The genesis of *Modern Times* is worth recalling here; Chaplin asserts that the film "started from an abstract idea, an impulse to say something about the way life is being standardised and channelised, and men turned into machines" (Ackroyd 182).

The conventional view of Chaplin's modern critics seems blindfolded to the Tramp's actions, which they perceive to be heroic—Peter Ackroyd refers to him affectionately as "the little hero of *Modern Times*"—but they are far from heroic (*Charlie Chaplin* 182). Nor are the Tramp and the gamine "joyous," really, when their plight is the focus in every scene and sequence they appear, and they struggle without knowing where they are in "modern times" (182). What, for example, is heroic in the way and manner he treats (and abuses) his colleague? Chaplin indeed "says something about the way life is being standardised" by depicting the Tramp as the victimizer who has become the machine. Moreover, Peter Ackroyd points to this obvious brutal reality underlying *Modern Times* when he asserts that "in a larger sense the factory represents the modern world in which the figure of the Little Tramp is perhaps obsolete; he generally represents a 'shabby-genteel' figure from the turn of the century. So he tried to reinvent himself as a worker on the production line" (186). The fact of the matter is that Chaplin shows that his "Little Tramp" is *not* "obsolete" in modern times—he is brutal; forced into brutal actions as banal as modern industrialized times demand. Even the Tramp's (and the film's) obsession with food is less an obsession about hunger than it is about "consumption." And we are all "consumers," there to be (ful)filled. If the Tramp is in any way heroic, it is because he—along with the gamine—represents the human individual becoming a relic of a time that devours people and discards them. We would do well to keep this point in mind when we come to the end of the film and its final tableaux of their shared open road.

Chaplin's character is an empty one—a naïve observer—a benign trope of modern life turned into an extension of itself. As soon as his associate is "liberated" from the machine, another strike occurs. The Tramp stands in the foreground with him and mimes his nuanced gestures. He proves that he is capable of mimicking any action. He clearly has not erased or elided "modern times," but in fact becomes its diabolical other. If the machine served as a sort of "womb" for the Tramp, as Parker Tyler asserts, then it is clear that the umbilical cord was never severed. He just feeds off modern times becoming in the process a mechanized version of them.

On his way out of the factory, the Tramp is repeatedly pushed away from the crowd of striking factory workers by a policeman—once again, he is alone—without solidarity. He inadvertently steps on a board which launches a brick at a police officer that strikes him in the head. He is taken to jail (again) for yet another inadvertent, misinterpreted accident. He is back in his comfort zone. He not only mimes the cruel world, he becomes it. It is not until the film's final acts that he will encounter a new world.

In *Think, Write, Speak*, the writer Vladimir Nabokov contends: "Chaplin is as good as Laurel and Hardy or Buster Keaton. But in terms of ideas, his genre as absolutely nothing to do with the comic art of literature, which is infinitely more complex than the art of the most refined clown" (371). Well, meanwhile . . . .

Notes

1 Chaplin Interviewed by Richard Meryman (1966), 9 Dec. 2019. https://scrapsfromtheloft.com/2019/12/09/chaplin-interview-richard-meryman-1966/
2 See Jason Demers' 2009 PhD thesis at York University, *Collecting Intensities: The Arrival of French Theory in America, 1970s*, in which he

> examine(s) the constellation of edited collections and special journal issues that emerged around the 1966 Johns Hopkins conference, focusing upon 1972—when the conference proceedings were republished under the title *The Structuralist Controversy*—as a banner year for publications on structuralism, particularly in the field of literary studies.

3 This is supported by Todd Phillips who reads their time together as romantic—they are on a date: "PROJECTED ON SCREEN, the Tramp roller skating blindfolded on a date with the Gamin (Paulette Goddard) in a department store." www.studiobinder.com/blog/joker-script-screenplay-pdf-download/
4 The Tramp is to Chaplin what the "gamine" is to Paulette Goddard—they are extensions of one another—the Tramp who calls to the gamine is equally Chaplin who calls to Goddard.
5 https://batman.fandom.com/wiki/Murray_Franklin
6 *Joker* Director Breaks Down the Opening Scene | Vanity Fair. www.youtube.com/watch?v=awoQuVq2yYc
7 David Robinson, in his commentary for the Criterion edition of the film, uses the words "fur coat."
8 "ModernTimes."www.loc.gov/static/programs/national-film-preservation-board/documents/modern_times.pdf

3 A comedian sees the world

Modern Times is Chaplin's astute insight into the industrial standardization of work and life. The film is a refocusing as well as a reframing act:

> I am tired of love and people and like all egocentrics, I turn to myself. I want to live in my youth again, to capture the moods and sensations of childhood, so remote from me now—so unreal—almost like a dream. I need to turn back time; to venture into the blurred past and bring it into focus.
>
> (*A Comedian Sees the World* 23)

At the end of the day, the film becomes an acerbic critique of the mechanical reproducibility of society in modern times, just as *The Great Dictator* becomes an acerbic critique of fascism as a form of authoritarianism already well underway when *Modern Times* was made. Both systems are, of course, comically inhumane to Chaplin, seen most clearly in that on seeing the famous Leni Riefenstahl film *The Triumph of the Will* (1935), his first and overwhelming reaction was to burst out laughing. It may very well have been his inspiration for his own *The Great Dictator* (1940). Chaplin did, after all, insist that he was not political at all (especially not socialist) but only wanted to make films.[1]

Even a casual glance at Chaplin's travel memoirs, *My Trip Abroad* (1922) and especially *A Comedian Sees the World* (1933), reveals his concern for the oppressed and outcast—"with depression and growing unemployment" in addition to "the rise of growing nationalism" (*A Comedian Sees the World* 61 and "Filming *Modern Times*" respectively); there we encounter a comedian who sees the effects of the socio-economic depression looming: "These things are bound to create trouble and it does not look as though conditions will improve" (66–67). "What's the use of trying?" asks the gamin at the end of *Modern Times* in 1936.

DOI: 10.4324/9780429323317-3

Miriam Bratu Hansen asserts: "Kracauer reads the happy endings of Chaplin's films as an injunction saying 'we must go on living' (MN, 2:33), an injunction that entails rethinking the conditions of experience, memory, and interaction after the catastrophe" (xxii). The final act grants us a privileged view of times to come. "The singing waiter" turns the film on its head. The moment he utters his first "word," *Modern Times*, the era of the silent film, is ended—becomes in that very moment an artifact of the historical past. The birth of this new reality comes at the cost of the death of the old; the mime who attempts to speak for the first time. Yet, in this moment, it is an uncivil discourse that he speaks—it is gibberish—"rapid and inarticulate speech"—"the language of rogues and gypsies."[2]

If we consider *Modern Times* comoedically, we discern a story that is a representation of the reality of "these modern times" as it is experienced and lived in the 1930s.[3] Speculating on the novel as a changing form, Robert Louis Stevenson, points out that "The novel, which is a work of art, exists, not by its resemblances to life, which are forced and material, but by its immeasurable difference from life."[4] Put in filmic terms, "life is a tragedy when seen in close-up," as Chaplin asserts, "but a comedy in long shot." And, "in some instances a long shot can effect greater emphasis" (*My Autobiography* 152).

If this is so, then *Modern Times* is about the work of life in the age of mechanical reproducibility. The lens through which we recognize reality is the same lens which recognizes our true natures; that the suffering of others can be an object of privileged amusement; that the suffering of others—tragic characters and events—can provide catharsis and can be understood in terms of tragedy which is commonly understood to relieve the audience of pity and fear. Can we say then that Chaplin allows his audience to indulge in "Schadenfreude"? Or, turning to the case of post-modern film like *Joker*, provide the audience with an entertaining *spectacle*? To answer these questions, we must come to the final act and scenes in *Modern Times*. The café sequences shine a light on the film as both a work in-the-making and unmaking, in addition to Chaplin's aesthetic of film.

Chaplin asserts that in his films he is trying to do something more than just comedy; "to bring to the coarse popular show of slapstick movies the subtler skills he had developed in the music halls and to 'add another dimension to my films besides that of comedy'" (David Robinson in *My Autobiography* 4). "I was beginning to think of comedy in a structural sense," Chaplin points out,

> and to become conscious of its architectural form. Each sequence implied the next sequence, all of them relating to the whole. If a gag

interfered with the logic of events, no matter how funny it was, I would not use it.

(*My Autobiography* 208)

The restaurant montage sequence is actually a reiteration of the opening scenes in the factory: we observe the Tramp at work—frustrated co-workers, agitated bosses—angry patrons replace innocent passers-by; accidents happen and beget accidents, culminating in a great escape in the final act; incarceration in the first. This time, however, both the gamine and the Tramp's escape succeeds—they are liberated and start anew. And in this sequence, the Tramp once again succumbs to—and is swallowed up by—the "machinery" and apparatus of film production. Chaplin, through the Tramp who "speaks" for the first time on film, acknowledges a sea change that the sonorization of cinema ushers in, but also a profound existential loss—"What's the use of trying?" says the gamine on having lost her first successful steady job. "Buck up—never say die. We'll get along!" is the Tramp's response. Chaplin not only presents life as we know it by "the outrageous absurdity of the situation or characters"; he draws parallels between film and lived experience—experience mediated through images, characters, accidents and events.

The "comoedic" is meant as the reversal of Aristotle's definition of "how to write" in his *Poetics*: in Tragedy, the characters exist for the purpose of "imitating an action," whereas in Comedy, the action exists for the purpose of "imitating characters" (creating caricatures) which inspire a temporary "pity and fear" (sympathy) for them among the audience, rather than providing the audience with "catharsis" from those emotions. Hence, Tragedy involves suffering, which is "an action that involves destruction or pain," but comedy is the polar opposite: "the laughable is an error or disgrace that does not involve pain or destruction" (*Poetics* lxii).

The final act, the café scene is not only a world-in-the-making but also a world-in-the-unmaking: it is a culmination of all the other episodes and takes us back to other scenes; moreover, it was an "afterthought."[5] The new ending problematizes the Tramp's innocence—mimes do not speak; and the Tramp, once he does speak, can never again be *the* iconic mime—and in this we can rely on Chaplin's text, *A Comedian Sees the World*. And when he does speak it is nonsense—gibberish. There is no "politics" in that—he is not making a statement; in fact, he goes out of his way to avoid making a statement. His decision to speak is aesthetic. For an artist like Chaplin who is sensitive to thinking as a verb, the artistic problem that he opens up is summed up in the life-changing question of "Where do I go from here?" David Robinson is right to point out that the film is not "Socialist ideology." It is, however, a critique of industrialization, and that critique extends into the socio-economy and chaos of the final acts: "The best ideas grow out of the situation . . . you cannot be funny without a funny situation. You can do something clownish, perhaps stumble, but you must have a funny situation" (Meryman 361). "Situation" engenders "world."

Clearly, Chaplin's extension of the comical into the realm of the comoedic, to borrow Kracauer's expression, "redeems physical reality," plunges us into the middle of everything and presents the world as it is—with indifference. The aesthetic of comoedic indifference—the sudden appearance of the commonplace in otherwise elevated manner or style, anticlimax; exceptional commonplaceness, triteness; insincere or overdone pathos or "mock sentimentalism"[6] alters, "if ever so slightly," "the relations, proportions, values" within the work—defamiliarizes the familiar. "Yet if we consider the highest order of life is the pursuit of the beautiful," Chaplin asserts, "what is more rational than applying it to the commonplace" (*A Comedian* 151–153)? Sergei Eisenstein writes,

> The work becomes organic and reaches the heights of genuine pathos only when the theme and content and idea of the work become an organic and continuous whole with the ideas, the feelings, with the very breath of the author. Then and only then will occur a genuine organic-ness of a work, which enters the circle of natural and social phenomena as a fellow-member with equal rights, as "an independent phenomenon."

The new—"really new"[7]—work alters the old and the whole tradition of existing works. Chaplin's "comoedic" breakthroughs can be linked to his economic speculations and hypotheses; the café montage sequence bears that out.

But the film goes deeper into the crisis of the times than if it were ideologically either for or against the Socialism or even the New Deal, heavily critiqued by Herbert Hoover as a form of "Socialism" at the time.

FDR's New Deal should be considered background to the film's clearly evident social conscience, but the art of the film is not ideological as such, no matter how closely it touches on the ideological conditions of the times. The New Deal was a set of social and economic reforms that had ideological roots in reforms of Capitalism represented by Social Democracy, Socialism and Communism, with which it shared much common moral ground.

Modern Times is of course a critique of the effect of the fearful modern times of the post–World War I period, culminating in the Depression. The film goes psychologically far more deeply into the crisis of those times than mere ideological critique—ideology is never funny. Chaplin's own economic position is clear-eyed in its time and for its time: in *A Comedian Sees the World*, he observes,

> The recovery of past economic depressions may have been due to inventions and new enterprises, but since those days the necessity of

man power has been rapidly decreasing because of modern machinery; and whatever new enterprises crop up in the future, they will not require the man power that was necessary in the past. Therefore, as man's only means of consuming what machinery produces is by work, our problem becomes a different one.

(69–70)

While the economic reality of *Modern Times* is asserted with a comoedic insight, the problem Chaplin foresees is discussed by Max Horkheimer and Theodor W. Adorno:

> The increase in economic productivity which creates the conditions for a more just world also affords the technical apparatus and the social groups controlling it a disproportionate advantage over the rest of the population. The individual is entirely nullified in face of the economic powers. These powers are taking society's domination over nature to unimagined heights. While individuals as such are vanishing before the apparatus they serve, they are provided for by that apparatus and better than before. In the unjust state of society the powerlessness and pliability of the masses increase with the quality of good allocated to them.
> (Horkheimer and Adorno 116–117)

"History today is not repeating itself," Chaplin points out in *A Comedian Sees the World* (61), since the controlling social groups include the Tramp's various employers in *Modern Times*; those social groups controlling the means of production are out of control and running amok. And not just the employers, but the larger fabric of society, including the authorities that mediate the relationship of employers to employees (and the un-[no longer]-employed, of course) seem themselves out of control—arbitrary. Chaplin's prophetic statements on economics "begin to shift the focus from politics to the signs of post-capitalism that are discernable within global capitalism itself" (*The Relevance of the Communist Manifesto* 3) And, as Slavoj Žižek who is representative of this kind of critique points out:

> we don't have to look far: the public figures who exemplify the privatization of our commons—Elon Musk, Bill Gates, Jeff Bezos, [and] Mark Zuckerberg, all "socially conscious" billionaires—leave bagfuls of warnings in their trail. They stand for global capital at its most seductive and "progressive"—in short, at its most dangerous. (In a speech to Harvard graduates in May 2017, Zuckerberg told his public: "Our job is to create a sense of purpose!" This comes from a man who,

with Facebook, has created the world's most expansive instrument of purposeless loss of time).

(2–3)[8]

Zuckerberg's comment, which Žižek cites, is designed to deflect the plight of the disenfranchised masses, but the masses begin pushing back in the film *Joker*, which we are reading here as the post-modern version of *Modern Times*: newspaper headlines in the *Gotham Times* in Phillips's film, for example, play on the spectator as a naïve observer and connote sinister subtexts: "Kill the Rich! A New Movement?" Sinister indeed—the question has become a populist movement in our current virtual post-modern sphere. *Joker*, although set in the neoconservative Thatcher-Reagan era of the 1980s, clearly also references the populist "Occupy" protest movements against the "1%" of their socio-economic policies empowered, beginning in 2011, eight years before Phillips made this film, collapsing the intervening 40 years into *post-modern times*.

At the end of *Modern Times*, the monotony of the factory is replaced with the chaos of the dance hall—we have transitioned from *Metropolis* inspired machinery to Brueghel-like scenes of uproarious crowds, the bustling busyness of the restaurant, embodied in the exasperated and indignant expressions of the irate patron ([Lloyd Ingraham] who happens to also resemble the authoritarian president of the Electro Steel Corporation in the opening scenes). His frenzied and frenetic hysteria fills the whole screen and conjures up the automated feeding machine—the system marches on and he becomes a metaphor of its abuses and violence; and, most significantly, the recorded and commanding voiceover that introduced J. Widdecombe Billows and his contraption parallels the spirited human voice of the Tramp who "speaks" for the first time in this final act. Furthermore, if the machine is a womb, as Parker Tyler envisions, a form of "mother," then the Tramp who feeds the trapped mechanic boss is its unfeeling midwife who is born in the opening scenes in the factory. Saul Austerlitz comments that "*Modern Times* is actually, secretly, an origin story for the Tramp, just in time for his farewell.[9] When Charlie is hired as a singing waiter and belts out a charming gibberish song composed of jumbled, faux-Italian syllables—[we witness] Chaplin's virgin attempt at producing sound, if not speech, on-screen—and we are witnessing the birth of an entertainer. All that has passed," he contends, "is mere prologue. But the singing Tramp would not go on." The Tramp's performance, then, becomes self-reflective pathos, which is "life" in the raw. But the sequence, which begins again on the street, is also the "gamine's" origin story: she performs in the street, outside the Red Moon Café adjacent to children who ride the carousel, close to the waterfront. This context takes us back to where she also originally began.

David Robinson points out that among

> the sequences that were to be rejected was a long scene of slapstick action when Charlie pretends he is a qualified steam shovel operator in order to get a job. In another sequence Charlie and the Gamin take shelter in an empty house, unaware that it is in the process of being demolished.
>
> (*Chaplin: His Life and Art* 462)

Furthermore, Robinson comments:

> Chaplin's politico-economic preoccupations surface in a scene in which Charlie and the girl are punished for eating eggs which are being dumped in the sea as surplus. [And in another rejected scene CP], the Gamin steals purses and wallets, which Charlie politely returns hoping for (but not demanding) a reward from the grateful owners. The café sequence in this draft is very different: it is Charlie who first gets a job as a waiter, and in turn gets a place for the girl—in blissful innocence that the place is also used as a bawdy house.
>
> (462)

In any case, there is a semblance or remainder of each of these discarded scenarios in the film's final cut. The "steam shovel operator" gag surfaces near the end of *Modern Times* when the Tramp is hired on by the "Jetson Mill" as a mechanic's assistant; the abandoned "empty house" under demolition surfaces as the gamine's ramshackle shack. And the scenarios featuring "surplus" food come in just before the Tramp collides with the gamine in the street when he eats an excessive amount in a cafeteria without paying, and "Charlie politely" returning purses and wallets reminds us of the scene in the jail when he foils a jailbreak and politely returns the prison cell keys. This last idea also reminds us of the Tramp returning the bread that the gamine stole. These gag ideas are all rooted in the film's original working titles which included "The Masses" and "The Commonwealth," subjects that pervade the *Modern Times* with its ironic thematics of common welfare and the common good.

Moreover, in the planned original ending, the Tramp suffers a nervous breakdown; he is visited by the "gamine" who has now become a nun. If the past is "mere prologue" for the future, then the revised ending is now the mere present. If *Modern Times* concludes at all on a utopian scene, it is utopian in the sense that we come to see the gamine and Tramp as equal;

however, they are present to each other; they are on a new road—a divided highway, on which traffic runs both towards and away from the point of view of the audience. Neither the viewer nor the couple know the future. They—together—become an example for life in art at the end, and their example instructs Chaplin, the author. The Tramp has broken the barrier of silence and produces vocalized sound. Both, just as the Tramp has countless times before, walk a familiar path into an unknown and uncertain future; it is a candid ending and conclusion to a film that sees its creator grappling with the relationship of silent film and "talkies." The gamine's hesitation—"What's the use of trying"—does not affect the Tramp's resolve to accept what their future might bring. It is a touching moment, indeed, but the smile he puts on is merely half a smile—"We'll get along"—he doesn't really believe it. But the Tramp's "reassurance" is also a comfort to Chaplin, the Tramp's creator. He has put the Tramp in every situation imaginable from art to social and political life. The planned original ending would have had history reverse itself. The final cut for the ending opens up to an undetermined future history.

Chaplin's conversation with Albert Einstein inspired his most straightforward and prescient remarks on social economics, his meeting with Winston Churchill and his most illuminating and terse affirmation of the comoedic: "This is not alone clever psychology. It is action and fun" (*A Comedian* 58). In 1933, comedies "were only an excuse for a chase," Chaplin elaborates, "but I wanted to stand still and be funny" (*A Comedian* 99–100). We are reminded of Chaplin's plain but paramount observation that "Pictures are pantomimic art." Chaplin seems to purposefully betray his own aesthetic by having the Tramp "speak." However, the character of the Tramp as a mime is restored in the film's closing scene when he interacts with the sad gamine and performs his final gesture, a half-smile, as the score in the background for the film plays "Smile"—a song Chaplin composed specifically for *Modern Times*.[10]

Chaplin, as David Robinson points out, "planned to prepare for the ending with a recurrent theme of a kindly nun, and her effect upon the Gamin" (*Chaplin: His Life and Art* 467); he intended the character of the nun to foreground "a momentary feeling or sense of beauty," a plot device that has its origin in a reflection expressed by Maurice Maeterlinck which Chaplin documents in *A Comedian Sees the World* in 1933:

> There comes a moment in life when moral beauty seems more urgent, more penetrating, than intellectual beauty; when all that the mind has treasured must be bathed in the greatness of soul, lest it perish in the sandy desert, forlorn as the river that seeks in vain for the sea.
> (96–97)

Chaplin intended the original ending to develop from this scenario or theme which he numbered—it was important to him:

1. On one of our adventures, we come into contact with a nun. It's just a momentary feeling or sense of beauty and the Gamin is moved by it. Gamin: "She makes me want to cry." The nun is always very tender and nice to the Gamin—a pat on the hand, etc.
2. We encounter her in the street again. The Gamin imitates her headgear and admires it. Each time the Gamin sees her she stops in the midst of the comedy and her eyes fill with tears and she says: "She makes me feel wicked."
3. We are in the street and the Gamin has just pinched something. The nun comes around the corner and the Gamin puts it back. [Charlie]: "What in blazes is wrong with you?" Gamin: (Gulp) "I dunno."

(*Chaplin: His Art and Life* 467–468)

We can see from this scenario that Chaplin is reaching for some kind of moral beauty; however, his strong retort—"What in blazes is wrong with you"—brings the metaphysical down to earth. The original penultimate scene would have the two together, parting ways:

> The scene changes to a hospital. Fully recovered, the Tramp, who is about to be discharged, is informed that a visitor is waiting to see him in the reception room. He makes his way, laboriously, towards it. When he arrives there, to his surprise, he finds the Gamin, attired as a nun. She is standing, and beside her is a Mother Superior. The Gamin greets him, smiling wistfully. The Tramp looks bewildered. Somehow a barrier has risen up between them. He tries to speak but can say nothing. Smiling sympathetically, she takes his hand. "You have been very ill," she says, "and now you are going out into the world again. Do take care of yourself, and remember I shall always like to hear from you."
>
> He tries to speak again but, with a gesture, gives it up. As she smiles, tears well up in her eyes while she holds his hand and he becomes embarrassed; then she stands [sic] as a final gesture that they must part.
>
> (462–463)

This description can remind us of the scene in the warden's office when the Tramp waits with the minister's wife. That scene is not intimate; however, it still retains a semblance of moral authority against a background of law and order. The "original" scenario and theme outlined previously is not intimate either, but clinical, clerical, and antiseptic; in a word, hopeless. Underlying its morality is the theme of "innocent, pure" (unrequited) love of previous historical times.

In regard to moral and intellectual beauty, we might re-evaluate this planned original ending of the film and compare it with the actual version produced in the final cut. The contrast between the two endings could not be more polarizing. In the original version, the Tramp "tries to speak"; in the ending, we have, however, he must speak—having put himself in a situation to speak—and he is helped along by the gamine. The original ending is "sadly sentimental" and "abandoned in favour of a more cheerful finale," as David Robinson comments, with "the couple, arm in arm, [setting] bravely off down a country lane, towards the horizon."[11] But Robinson is mistaken about this, too. It is not a "country lane," as Robinson calls it, but a divided highway. Chaplin films them together on this divided highway walking towards where we are and then they turn. They now walk away from us—we are now behind them—towards the vanishing point with the (imaginary) traffic running both towards and away from the audience into the future. It is a solid white line and not a broken one; for now, they are each in their own lane. Hardly a happy ending and calling it "cheerful" elides the reality of the look of palpable despair on the gamine's face. And this time "Ellen Peterson" wears the dress, hat and shoes of a working woman—she's moving up in the world. The original ending may have satisfied audiences, giving them the nostalgic ending they wanted: a silent Tramp intact and an assurance that the iconic mime will live on to fight another day. But how could he survive, let alone endure, in the post-modern world of sound—and with caricatures like Arthur Fleck coming at him? Of course, Chaplin always knew and understood the answer to the question about the Tramp's place in post-modern film:

> I don't think there's any place for that sort of person now. The world has become a little bit more ordered. I don't think it's happier now, by any means. I've noticed the kids with their short clothes and their long hair, and I think some of them want to be tramps. But there's not the same humility now. They don't know what humility is, so it has become something of an antique. It belongs to another era. That's why I couldn't do anything like that now. And, of course, sound—that's another reason. When talk came in I couldn't have my character at all. I wouldn't know what kind of voice he would have. So he had to go.
> (Meryman 360–361)

The original ending may have also satisfied, at first, a longing to resuscitate a spirituality as a form of innocence or "moral beauty" displaced if not lost by *Modern Times*; and certainly annihilated in *Joker* (*A Comedian Sees the*

World 87). But we know that Chaplin does not perform to audiences, that an audience for him, like the outstanding ending of *Modern Times* that we have, as it turns out, is an afterthought. He chooses to end the Tramp by preserving the authenticity of the sign—the gesture of the pantomime—while at the same time, he radically transforms our perception of the character by making him "sing" in gibberish. The break from silent mime to a singing waiter in a crowded and bustling café enacts a profound semantic and aesthetic shift in the film. We can turn for support for the authenticity of Chaplin's ending to Victor Shklovsky, who admires and uses Chaplin, for insight about works of art like *Modern Times* that subvert and undermine expectation and convention:

> A poet removes the sign from a thing and turns it sideways. Things rebel, they shed their old names and, with new ones, they take on a new configuration. A poet performs a semantic shift: he snatches a concept from the set in which it is usually kept, and with the aid of a word (trope), relocates it to a different semantic set, so that we experience the novelty of the sensation one derives from locating the thing in a new set.
>
> This is one of the means by which a palpable thing is created. In an image we have: an object—the memory of its former name, its new name, and the associations connected with the new name.
>
> (*Literature and Cinematography* 14)

Perhaps, Shklovsky could have had in mind the scene in *Modern Times* when the Tramp retrieves a red flag that has fallen off a lorry which comes to be mistaken for the Tramp's unwelcome and mistaken ideological position in the march. But the moment he speaks in the restaurant where he is also a waiter, he resurfaces as a new "trope"—"a new configuration" and a post-modern one—within his own modern silent film. The moment the Tramp speaks, the contemporary and the future enter into the film and the future itself becomes more fully present in the final scene—and is integrated as a part of the overall construction of the film. The "semantic shift" that occurs the moment the Tramp speaks enacts a radical transformation of the character—the literal death of the mime is not in vain. And he will resurface yet again in Todd Phillips's film *Joker* and in the character "Arthur Fleck." In many ways, *Joker* recalls the "original ending" of *Modern Times*. It opens with a theft and an assault.

Perhaps, it was Chaplin's intent that the "recurrent theme of a kindly nun" in a dark film about everyday work and life in "modern times" would remind spectators, nonetheless, of a hope and reward beyond the drudgery of everyday modern life—that real happiness resides beyond the reality of work and life's challenges and hardships; in reality, the original scenario that was planned as a moral ending to the film is sterile, reactionary and barren. It foregrounds the notion of a forced and contrived salvation—embodied most clearly in the "Mother Superior" figure who stands over and above and overwhelms the gamine-nun—through suffering and aloneness. This device would have placed the whole notion of "moral beauty" in the past—modern times are, after all about the death of God, the death of the past, if anything at all. But Chaplin chose to end the film—and the character of the Tramp as a mime—with a bang and not a whimper; he will endure and the gamine will endure, but as something else, down the road, in the undisclosed future. He is not alone at the end of the film nor is the gamine. And in a final farewell to his life as a mime, Chaplin photographs the pair in high contrast walking away, becoming smaller and more distant from us: they become two dimensional silhouettes against the open road and sky. What would have become of him trapped in a silent ending with no future? In direct contrast to this, Chaplin gives us an ending that preserves the struggle—which we relate to—that shows life being lived, the past being left behind and a future being faced. The closing image of *Modern Times* shows the Tramp and his companion giving the future a chance.

The separation and conflict between capital and labour and how it results in the creation of the hungry, the homeless and the unemployed is the dominant theme in *Modern Times*; not sin, guilt and salvation. The unhappy nun in the original ending scenario of *Modern Times* would have been a "Hollywood" ending: the wages of sin are suffering and damnation—hope lies in another world. Happily, for us, Chaplin chose a more critically sensitive ambiguous ending, rather than a "moral" one. To extend and elaborate on this critique further, one can turn to Christopher Nolan's interpretation of the "Joker" trope in his (2012) film *The Dark Knight Rises*. It fits well in between the comoedic *Modern Times* and the darker, depressive and more violent *Joker*. Nolan's film precedes *Joker* by only seven years, and it is visually closer to the comic book. The characters in *Joker*—especially Arthur Fleck—take post-modern times further: they see through but internalize the indifference, depravity and violence of their age. There will be no happy ending here.

Early in the film *The Dark Knight Rises*, Selina [Ann Hathaway] whispers to [Bruce] Wayne [Thomas Wayne's son] while they are dancing at an exclusive upper-class gala:

> A storm is coming, Mr. Wayne. You and your friends better batten down the hatches. Because when it hits, you're all going to wonder

how you thought you could live so large, and leave so little for the rest of us.

Such an encounter in *The Dark Knight Rises* cannot go unnoticed—it has a history—*Modern Times*. Slavoj Žižek elaborates on the significance of their encounter in *The Dark Knight Rises*. "Jonathan Nolan, Christopher Nolan's brother who co-wrote the scenario," Žižek comments, "is (as is every good liberal) 'worried' about the disparity and he admits this worry pervades the film." Further, Žižek, citing Jonathan Nolan, asserts:

> What I see in the film that relates to the real world is the idea of dishonesty. The film is all about that coming to a head . . . The notion of economic fairness creeps into the film, and the reason is twofold. One, Bruce Wayne is a billionaire. It has to be addressed . . . But two, there are a lot of things in life, and economics is one of them, where we have to take a lot of what we are told on trust, because most of us feel like we don't have the analytical tools to know what's going on . . . I don't feel there's a left or right perspective in the film. What is there is just an honest assessment or honest exploration of the world we live in— things that worry us.
>
> (*Trouble in Paradise* 196)

What "comes to a head" in Nolan's film originates in *Modern Times*; together, all three films—*Modern Times, The Dark Knight Rises* and *Joker*—show the characters undergoing trials and enduring them—the journey to the Hell and back. Chaplin can be said to lead his Tramp-figure on a journey and at the end, he and the gamine become human.

A photograph by Lee Miller published in Chaplin's *A Comedian Sees the World* shows him nearly in full, elevated, profile underneath an ornate chandelier. The image itself is a good example of comoedic art. The branching lights—there are four—that flood the film-maker's face signify both a talon on the one hand and a laurel crown on the other hand. It is difficult to discern if Chaplin is balancing the light fixture on his head or, by photographic foreshortening, has raised himself up to the ceiling; in any case, the assemblage is seamless. Clearly, however, this staged gesture references a comoedic sequence in *Modern Times* that includes the Tramp's at first futile effort serving a patron in the café the dish of roast duck. In the scene, the Tramp negotiates his way through crowds carrying the tray with the roast duck, right arm outstretched above his head until the duck is caught — "hooked"—on a dangling iron arm of a decorative chandelier resembling the one in Lee Miller's photograph. This seemingly innocuous gag recalls the earlier scene in the factory when, as a factory worker, he fastens himself to an iron hook in an effort to keep above the fray and the mayhem that he's just created, in a system that wants to "lynch," break and tame him even more to conform. The photograph offers an insight into the singular theme of *Modern Times*—eat or be eaten. The café sequence takes from all the other scenes of the crowds and the spectacles; and like many other scenes in *Modern Times*, it foregrounds the larger fabric of social authority that mediates the relationship of employers to employees and resituates them in one enclosed space.[12] A closer look at the Tramp's enraged patron will illuminate how the action exists for the purpose of creating caricatures; naturally, Chaplin keeps us at a measured and unwavering distance from the action or scene—comedy works in a long shot. These scenes are closer to the comoedic because they show aspects of modern life in a way that is contrary to the tragedy of modern times. Multiple scenes happen as if in an assemblage that vary from one act to the next; like the street scenes of speeding cars and the passers-by, each part is indifferent to other parts, and each scene is indifferent to every other. The anger and frustration of the patron directed towards his server also reminds us of the abuse the Tramp experienced in the factory, the authoritarian Capitalist-owner-president, and to the automation of everyday life, including the lunch hour. Here, in the café, the Tramp has a job to do. Yet, getting it done reiterates the opening images of the film: herded sheep and the lines of assembly line workers entering the social machinery of automation and production get in the way. They are voiceless in their sameness—the scene speaks for them—but are also harbingers of social unrest, violence and chaos in rebellion against the industrial means of production and their emerging place in the work force as mere commodities.

According to Chaplin, both the Tramp and his gamine are "The only two live spirits in a world of automatons. We are children," he contends, "with no sense of responsibility, whereas the rest of humanity is weighed down with duty. We are spiritually free."[13] This terse description, when one reads the scene (and scenes) in the restaurant, leads to a misconception of the characters as innocent, romantic, anarchic and subversive and as somehow aloof from the machinery that plagues them. Chaplin "shows" the scene—it takes on a life of its own; or, more accurately, it takes on life as lived—and as such, undermines the characters' innocent and seemingly innocuous intentions and reactions. The Tramp is far from anarchic; he is, in a word, a (budding) sociopath. Thus, Chaplin's own description reveals a rage for innocence—"We are children"—which is a rage the Tramp acts out at every turn.

Chaplin's recollection of a bullfight that he attends in Paris provides an almost uncanny glimpse into his aesthetic of film, and the darker sociopolitical aspects of *Modern Times*.

> A most beautiful yet revolting afternoon was spent at a bullfight in San Sebastian. For thrills and drama it excels any sport I've seen. On the

other hand, its sanguine brutality disgusts one. I had been told much about the technique of the bull fight—the beauty of the dance of death
Everything is ready for action

The matador, the killer, stands studying the bull, looking for bad habits. Then he takes him in hand, for he is the artist, the expert with the cape.

This is the *pièce de résistance*. This is the ballet, the dance, in which the fury of the bull is controlled and merged into beautiful plastic design.

The bull is all fury, circling around the man, obeying the dictates of the cape. Both merge into a sculptural unit. The horn scrapes the man's chest, taking with it a piece of gold braid. Everyone holds his breath until the matador, with a flourish of his cape, dismisses the bull and saunters away, giving him over to the toreadors, who keep him occupied until the picadors arrive.

The popular resentment among foreigners witnessing bullfighting is the cruelty to horses. As a matter of fact, these wretched animals are half-dead before they enter the ring. I asked a Spaniard why it was necessary to use the poor creatures. "A bull must have one triumph while he's in the arena," he said.

(*A Comedian* 115–116)

Chaplin's recollection illuminates how the comedian sees the world—literally; *Modern Times* illuminates how he presents the world as it is lived in a work of art—"this art means this life."[14] The emphasis, here, is on "this" as the present tense, which Chaplin demonstrates and foregrounds in *Modern Times*. Arthur Fleck, in *Joker*, however, makes *Modern Times* the past—his (and our) present is the post-modern. And for both Chaplin and the Tramp, *Modern Times* means "this" life; yet from the vantage point of Todd Phillips' film, it means "that" life—back then—in historical time. Moreover, in *Modern Times*, Chaplin's experiences and life are "the preliminary project of his future work. The work to come is hinted at."[15] The scene Chaplin describes is far from "comic." The Tramp, of course, is neither an "expert" nor an "artist" since both art and expertise require skill and intentionality. He is doing none of these things; rather, he is depicted as looking at life, not art. But he's doing so in a work of art: "This is the *pièce de résistance*. This is the ballet, the dance, in which the fury of the bull is controlled and merged into beautiful plastic design." *Modern Times* consists of one subversion after another—the sudden appearance of the commonplace in otherwise elevated manner or style, anticlimax, exceptional commonplaceness, triteness, insincere or overdone pathos and sentimentalism. This is the methodology of the comoedic, since what makes the subversion comic rather than tragic is the reality of "indifference." And the Tramp is indifferent to everything and everyone, except the gamine, and even that interest is self-serving; moreover, it would be too easy to compare the Tramp's actions to those of the bull. The Tramp is the other of the bull—part man ("killer"), part animal—"The bull is all fury, circling around the man, obeying the dictates of the cape. Both merge into a sculptural unit." The Tramp learns from "modern times" how to be inhuman, mechanical and uncaring—to step out of the dance of death. What stands out in Chaplin's recollection of the bullfight is the utterly cruel stupidity of the ritual illuminated by the Spaniard's comment when he is asked about the horses: "A bull must have one triumph while he's in the arena." His comment also can take us back and remind us of the opening scenes in the factory where the Tramp, overwhelmed by the oppressively repetitive work on the assembly line, runs amok yielding wrenches as horns on his head imitating Pan, the Greek God of shepherds and flocks. Indeed, *panning* from one shot to the next, out of the frying pan into the fire. In this early scene, violence is done to him and we do not yet take to heart the idea that it could come to reside in him; however, as the story develops, we begin to see that there is violence in the Tramp, a violence constantly ascribed to him, however mistakenly, by his environment.

The cinematic distance that Chaplin constructs in his films is provided to us, the viewers, his spectators, so that we can "think"—he shows us thinking. In his statements, he criticizes films that "don't think"; and thinking with the film illuminates Chaplin's double: author and Tramp. The Tramp, however, is incapable of distancing himself from the mayhem and violence he sees, but this is the joke. It is up to his audience to consider his relationship to the whole.

We can see how the spectator-viewer becomes a "thought-figure" in the café sequence; the enraged patron succeeds at playing the enraged bull, but there are other bulls in this arena and the Tramp, too, succeeds for a while at avoiding, and in one instance, ignoring the patrons altogether. The palpable intolerance of the angry café patron, however, follows the Tramp's every move; of all the "bit players" who seem to buzz around the Tramp like irritating flies, Lloyd Ingraham, the actor who plays the role, is the most ferocious.[16] Even the Tramp's "giant" co-worker at the Electro Steel Corporation in the opening sequence finds his humanity in the department store later in the film when he explains to a suddenly inebriated Tramp that he is not a burglar—"we're hungry"; and the Tramp's cellmate midway through the film has a "homey" side that is best expressed in his meticulous attention to his embroidery. But the angry patron cannot be redeemed—he is far from "loveable"—and he becomes a foil to the Tramp who can; the angry patron who seems violently unhappy demands his dinner while an incompetent waiter Tramp frustrates and aggravates those demands. One's experience of this angry patron is mediated through mostly "long shots." At one point, the enraged patron stands up on his chair screaming at the Tramp who is dominated by a crowd of carousing, indifferent guests. It might appear to the spectator that roles have been reversed—with the frustrated patron playing the role of a matador soliciting the attention of his frantic bull.

Ingraham's part in this final sequence act lasts no more than five minutes, during which time the Tramp is tripped by a dog on a leash—a comic image of a cultured domestic civility and reference back to the warden's office and the minister's wife and her little dog—astonishingly saving the tray of food and dishes that he carries, although he causes a collision between two other waiters when he enters through an "out" door into the cafe's kitchen. However, and this time he knows it, his innate indifference towards his co-workers manifests unambiguously. He is swept away by crowds that suddenly form—all the while "the waiter" never loses the roast duck he carries and balances on a tray above his head; however, he eventually loses it when it gets caught on the ornate hook of a chandelier, which then allows him to recover it and finally present it to the patron. And it is in this scene, finally, more than any other, that we experience the chaotic frustrations of modern times, with everything happening simultaneously, but producing nothing edible.

In the crowded scene, another group of four intoxicated patrons—three are uniformly dressed in pristine white football sweaters decorated with the letter "X," and another customer is dressed all in white, wearing a white hat, holding his little dog on a leash—the very dog that in the scene's opening shot tried to trip him. One of these "team mates" jests with the Tramp who is vigorously trying to carve up the duck, urging the Tramp to play a mock game by gesturing for a pass. Distracted by all the commotion the duck is jettisoned from beneath the Tramp's carving knife and fork, and a rugby-football match, using the roast duck as a football, breaks out. The duck is tossed from player to player; the Tramp finally catches it and is tackled, only to crash into his patron's table, where he finally presents the roast duck to him as "served."

In this absurd situation, the patron's fury remains directed at the Tramp. The Tramp as a waiter recalls once again the image of the defective feeding machine, in addition to "playing" the scene for an overdone pathos of loss. The Tramp works arduously at his job in this sequence, but the more he seems to work, the more he elides the task at hand; the more he irritates his affluent patron, the more his guest becomes agitated. The patron is a snob; his reactions, disdainful. Life as it is experienced in the restaurant represents the social ethos and temper of class-consciousness in these "modern times." "Snobbishness," Chaplin comments, is the national fault of all countries. Republics are the same. Take America—for example, its social register and its exclusive clubs, busy excluding. Your occupations and your sports come under a snobbish category. If you can claim to generations of polo-playing in your family, your social position is usually unassailable.

(*A Comedian Sees the World* 30)

Nicholas Barber, in an essay on the eightieth anniversary of the release of Chaplin's film, *The Great Dictator*, writes: "The Great Dictator is a masterpiece that isn't just a delightful comedy and a grim agitprop drama, but a spookily accurate insight into Hitler's psychology." And, citing the Greek-French film director Costa-Gavras,[17] Barber underscores Chaplin's artistic and mental courage: "He was a visionary. He saw the future while the leaders of the world couldn't see it." ("The Great Dictator: The film that dared to laugh at Hitler").[18] "To me," Chaplin contends, "the funniest thing in the world is to ridicule impostors" (Barber). Barber points out that the film

> has been accused of trivialising Nazi atrocities. Chaplin himself writes, in his autobiography, "Had I known the actual horrors of the German concentration camps, I could not have made *The Great Dictator*; I could not have made fun of the homicidal insanity of the Nazis." But he isn't just making fun of Hitler—as Mel Brooks did in *The Producers* in 1967—*he is making an astute point about the fragile egos of male world leaders*.

(emphasis added)

We can surmise that Lloyd Ingraham's performance in *Modern Times*—his inflated expressions, shouting, rapid and mechanical gestures—is the "idea" upon which Chaplin's dictator is constructed.

Barber's observation represents the conventional view of the Tramp, but now we see the figure in relation to dictators in modern times. "Each has mirrored the same reality—the predicament of the 'little man' in modern society," he avers. "Each is a distorting mirror, the one for good, the other for untold evil." The banality of Hitler's evil is not untouchable or beyond human understanding; nor is the Tramp's "good" untouchable perfect, or sacrosanct. Hitler was kind to animals; the Tramp was not. At least that is what spectators see when they see comoedically through the indifferent lens of the Tramp and his condition in these "modern times." Perhaps by "good" Barber means indifference to good—the *comoedic*.

The final act of *Modern Times* stands out for other reasons. Its final scenes present the gamine in a way that recalls her transformation from "gamine" to "celebrity" in the department store sequence. The sequence of scenes now opens with her waiting for the Tramp at a familiar place—outside the police station near a street corner. She has raised herself up in class status as her dress shows us, as well as her purse which now contains money; and she has found some "class" for herself. In a short scene that functions almost like an intertitle lasting only seconds by cutting in-between helping him get hired—she speaks for him—they have joined forces. Her small black purse, which she displays in front of him, is a sign that their roles have turned. He puts his hands on her and spins her around in a manner that recalls her display in the department store and her street dancing moments earlier. She has become a sex object.[19] Staged reality is suddenly on display once again.

The Tramp's transformation into the "singing waiter" is the final act's most outstanding and breathtaking intervention. His performance ushers in the new times awaiting "Chaplin" and his characters. Two truancy officers are waiting for the gamine in the audience; they seize her immediately following the Tramp's performance; the *maître d*—himself a kind of *matador* for the Tramp—is summoned, and for the first time, we are shown the gamine's full name as it is written on her "wanted" notice-poster-pamphlet: "Ellen Peterson." They try to take her into custody and there is a struggle: two men against one "gamine." What kind of comedy are the spectators now witness to?

"Comedy," Aristotle points out in his *Poetics*, is

> "an imitation of inferior people—not, however, with respect to every kind of defect: the laughable is a species of what is disgraceful. The laughable is an error or disgrace that does not involve pain or destruction; for example, a comic mask is ugly and distorted, but does not involve pain" (*Poetics* 9)—"life in long shot."

"Our tragedies," Chaplin opines, "are only as big as we make them" (*A Comedian Sees the World* 30). Moreover, Malcolm Heath notes that the word

> "inferior" has both moral and social implications. The central figures of comedy will include the lowly persons (such as peasants and slaves) who are only peripheral in tragedy; and comic characters, even those of high status, will tend to behave badly.
>
> (*Poetics* lxii)

We have already seen that. However, in this character-transforming sequence Chaplin gives Aristotle a run for his money.

The notion of the formerly silent Tramp, who becomes the singing waiter, negotiating his way about the crowded café, is itself a comical idea. Chaplin changes the camera's point of view. The spectator becomes a patron.

The Tramp's Dada-inspired rendition of Léo Daniderff's "Je cherche après Titine" ("I am looking for Titine," with its emphasis on the diminutive form of feminine names) is both blindsiding and eye-opening—it is a comical song about a special kind of seduction—"A pretty girl and a gay old man."

Many critics, such as Siegfried Kracauer, have seen in the Tramp's struggles a metaphor for the Biblical myth of David and Goliath.[20] But he is no David; he is no "Superman." In fact, the Tramp is more like Saul who, in the Biblical story of Israel, turns out to be an incompetent and unfit ruler. It is even more of a strain to accept that the Tramp is an underdog; underdogs are not necessarily valueless, but black sheep are; moreover, we already know that any success that comes the Tramp's way is both incidental and accidental. Chaplin uses popular tropes in literal ways; he avoids making popular films, a phrase that we should extrapolate: in *My Autobiography*, Chaplin touches on the rationale behind popular films. "The theme of most of these spectacles is Superman," he asserts. "The hero can out-jump, out-climb, out-shoot, out-fight and out-love anyone in the picture. In fact every human problem is solved by these methods—*except thinking*" (*My Autobiography* 251; emphasis added). This is at first sight a strange comment since the Tramp, as Siegfried Kracauer illuminates in his seminal study, *Theory of Film*, is "indestructible," and always (eventually, ultimately) "out-jumps," "out-climbs," "out-fights" and "out-loves" nearly every other character he comes in contact with—but he does so inadvertently, accidentally—that's always the joke.

In this last sequence in *Modern Times*, the previously silent Tramp out-performs, out-*thinks* and even *out-speaks* everyone else. He is indestructible because he is singular of purpose, not because he is "everyman." And once again, accident and chance—in this instance, it is his inability to remember lyrics—reveal the true nature of his thought: *improvisation*—the staged is made to look unstaged.

Of course, the Tramp "forgets"[21] the lyric—the plot of a story that he has (sort of) lived but cannot admit to; moreover, the audience is reminded of what or who has become the object of his almost singular "pursuit"—"Ellen." The lyrics of his song amount to a confession (Figure 3.1).

"The accompanying pantomime elaborates a tale of a seducer and a coyly young maiden"—"gamine" (*Chaplin: His Life and Art* 468). We see the emphasis on improvisation in an early exchange with the writer H.G. Wells who gives insight into Chaplin's aesthetic, creative process and comoedic world view.

> Wells comments on my dapperness as he helps me on with my coat. "I see you have a cane with you." I was also wearing a silk hat. I wondered

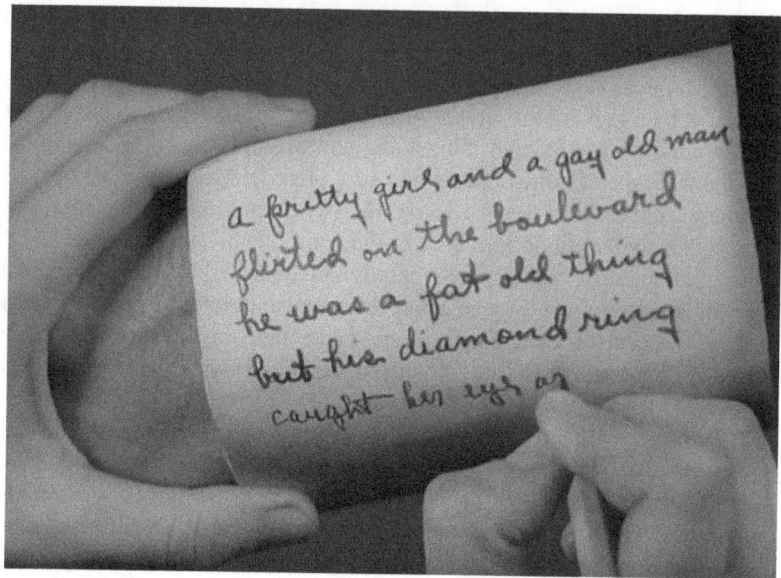

Figure 3.1 "A pretty girl and a gay old man"

what Los Angeles and Hollywood would say if I paraded there in this costume?

Wells tries on my hat, then takes my cane and twirls it. The effect is ridiculous, especially as just at that moment I notice two volumes of the *Outline of History* on his table.

Strutting stagily, he chants, "You're quite the fellow, doncher know." We both laugh. Another virtue for Wells. He's human.

I try to explain my dress. Tell him that it is my other self, a reaction from the everyday Chaplin. I have always desired to look natty and I have spurts of primness. Everything about me and my work is so sensual that I must get reaction. My dress is part of it. I feel that it is a poor explanation of the paradox, but Wells thinks otherwise.

(*My Wonderful Visit* 128–129)

In the experience remembered earlier, an everyday occurrence becomes both the subject and the material for staged reality, but the focus in the scenario-performance is always "human" nature. In the spellbinding final moment in his final performance in *Modern Times*, we do not know what the Tramp will do or what he is thinking, even though the gamine had written it all out for him—and us, the spectator outside of the film—moments before. Let us assume, then, that the lyric written out on his shirt cuff is itself a metaphor for history, and his past, which he loses in a dramatic moment ("event"). The loss renders us—the spectators—naïve, and we step out of history for an instant. The moment he attempts to speak the Tramp is no longer "historical." He freezes and looks around for the cuff, realizing suddenly that it is nowhere to be seen—he looks to the gamine like some "Beatrice."[22] This loss of the lyric is both mundane, an everyday occurrence, and profound; the scene builds up and includes us, making it our loss too, because we witnessed it, and even read it: Chaplin's camera gave us a close-up shot of the lyrics just seconds ago. Now, having lost them in his first proactive rather than reactive movement, the Tramp must improvise—and this is what he "remembers":

> Se bella piu satore, je notre so catore,
> Je notre qui cavore, je la qu', la qui, la quai!
> Le spinash or le busho, cigaretto toto bello,
> Ce rakish spagoletto, si la tu, la tu, la tua!
> Senora pelafima, voulez-vous le taximeter,
> La zionta sur le tita, tu le tu le tu le wa!
> and so on for several more stanzas.
> (*Chaplin: His Life and Art* 468)

But the Tramp's "language" is gibberish: nonsense. It is an *imitation of language* that now references and reimagines the silent past of the Tramp apposite his stillbirth in sound film; in this anticlimactic moment, Chaplin "redeems" the pantomimic art and praxis of the Tramp by annunciating his death: what we hear is not what we want to hear. His choreography and movement destroys and reconstructs both his and our frame of reference intruded on by sound, utterance and otherness: "What happens," as Ann Lauterbach noted, "if the frame breaks and this thing, this otherness, gets inside? Doesn't everything change, the frame as well as each thing it once held apart?"

A revealing and dramatic analogy for the kind of thinking and aesthetic can be imagined and illustrated by our referring to Paul Klee's (1920) monoprint, *Angelus Novus*, which Walter Benjamin sees in this light:

> There is a painting by Klee called Angelus Novus. An angel is depicted there who looks as though he were about to distance himself from something which he is staring at. His eyes are opened wide, his mouth stands open and his wings are outstretched. The Angel of History must look just so. His face is turned towards the past. Where *we* see the

appearance of a chain of events, *he* sees one single catastrophe, which unceasingly piles rubble on top of rubble and hurls it before his feet. He would like to pause for a moment so fair [*verweilen*: a reference to Goethe's Faust], to awaken the dead and to piece together what has been smashed. But a storm is blowing from Paradise, it has caught itself up in his wings and is so strong that the Angel can no longer close them. The storm drives him irresistibly into the future, to which his back is turned, while the rubble-heap before him grows sky-high. That which we call progress, is *this* storm.

Chaplin sees that we are blinded by the historical fantasy of "progress," but Klee's picture sees history—the past—as a single predictable narrative in which the victim is arrested in time or a "state of emergency."

There are similarities which can be drawn between the Tramp's final performance and comportment and Klee's new angel. The moment he speaks—"eyes staring," "mouth open"—the Tramp renders himself mute as the pantomime—the "Holy Innocent." His "innocence" was always in question, and now, stepping out of a modern silent film, he becomes something other—something "new," something "post-modern"—his face "turned toward the past"—the gamine who hides offstage in her new role as the Tramp's "tutor." He is the centre of attention now, as he forgets his lines that he was practising with her just moments before; now, brought to a new reality, Chaplin's frozen stance, repeated again and again, performs in the face of that forgetting: he hesitates—he is about to speak—to sing, no less. Of course we don't know that—nothing is certain—although we listen for it with our eyes. Thus, he hesitates and in this frozen moment of apprehension we see, following Benjamin, "the same will to grasp the sense of the world or of history in its nascent state" (*The Stanford Philosophical Encyclopedia*). Forgetting implies thought, but the Tramp "makes whole what has been" lost. And just as in earlier episodes and scenes in which he uses the very technologies and techniques of mechanization and standardization of the machine age to create a facsimile of a life lived in the pathos of modernist reality, he begins to speak using a language that parodies his former image: "gibberish"—"talk in no known language"—"the language of rogues and gypsies."[23] Both Klee's figure of the angel and the Tramp when he speaks are anticlimactic performances: the angel freezes and the Tramp speaks in tongues. They need not do more to make us "think" and reflect, since "Thinking," as Walter Benjamin comments, "involves not only the flow of thoughts, but their arrest as well" ("On the Concept of History" 396). *Modern Times* is a dark film. The Tramp deconstructs speech into its phonetic parts jumbled together without meaning or syntax. Once more, he

A comedian sees the world 91

Figure 3.2 Singing waiter just before he is about to sing—his posture resembling Klee's angel

foregrounds and masters conflict before resolution. Chaplin leaves that for his viewer to discern (Figure 3.2).

Taking the final scene to another level of insight on "how the comedian sees the world," we see that Chaplin does here what he has always done: he keeps the spectator at arm's length. "The spectator is, so to speak," and to paraphrase Viktor Shklovsky, "moved away from" what is depicted (*Shklovsky Reader* 270). Shklovsky correctly cites Bertolt Brecht and contends that

> Brecht introduces into his theatre practice what he calls "the device of alienation," showing phenomenon of life and human types not in their usual form, but from a new, unexpected perspective, forcing one to actively take position toward them. The sense of this technique known as "the device of alienation," explains Brecht, "consists in inspiring the spectator to perceive the depicted events in an analytical, critical fashion."
> (270)

Chaplin's economic theory (quoted earlier) is here put to a test even in aesthetic terms: "History today is not repeating itself" (*A Comedian Sees the World* 61). The Tramp's performance is a total break with his past. Once voiced, the Tramp can no longer be the "Tramp"; at best, he can only finish the routine (the film) as expected (chaotically) and keep moving, which is exactly what he enacts at the end in the final shot: "But a storm is blowing from Paradise; it has got caught in his wings with such violence that the angel can no longer close them." The Tramp, once he opens his mouth, can no longer close it. Sound—not the song—"propels him into the future," having become fully the past, "to which his back is turned, while the pile of debris before him grows skyward" ("On the Concept of History" 392)—the future—*Fordism*, "slouching towards Bethlehem,"[24] coming to roost. He has become the storm. He is culpable. He is the other of Paul Klee's "angel." His innocence is a joke.

Likewise, in *Joker*—we witness the triumph of *Trumpism*.[25] And here, we might turn to the finale in *Joker*, which is saturated in the ethos of the era. That film's finale advances the Fordism of *Modern Times* by illustrating a theory of alienation whereby the working classes, instead of changing the conditions under which they labour and live, become passive in the face of apparently autonomous exchanges of commodities, which include themselves. And this time, the crowd is silent, muted for a moment as Fleck-turned pantomime dances, shot in slow motion, on the hood of a crashed police cruiser: "Still he keeps smiling as he wipes his hand from one cheek across his mouth to his other cheek."[26] Joker's "gesture" is no gesture at all, in contrast to the Tramp's, but a full smile made with both hands—it is a smile written in blood—which he tastes first with two fingers. Arthur Fleck's great failure is Joker's great success—now, he has an audience and he performs before it. The stage is set. We see him next in an interrogation room in the Arkham State Hospital with his psychiatrist. His laugh is almost mechanical, yet "That laugh in that scene is really the only time he laughs genuinely," Phillips says.

> There are different laughs in the movie. There is the laugh from Arthur's affliction and then there is his fake laugh when he's trying to be "one of the people," which is my favorite laugh. But at the end, when he's in the room at Arkham State Hospital, that's his only genuine laugh in the movie.

And this is where we might also consider Arthur Fleck's story a continuation of *Modern Times*—the future as we have already observed is unknown for the couple—the Tramp and gamine—brought together by accident but choosing now to face it together. One possible scenario is that they enter a new world—the world of Arthur Fleck and post-modern times. History will not be on their side.

HOSPITAL DOCTOR: What's so funny?
[He takes a deep breath, his eyes are glazed over. His voice is scratchy, like he doesn't use it much. But the smile never leaves his crooked lips.]
JOKER: —just thinking of this joke.
HOSPITAL DOCTOR: Do you want to tell it to me?
JOKER: You wouldn't get it.[27]

In the end, the joke is on us, the audience. Phillips has said that one of the main influences on his film was *The Killing Joke*, the acclaimed 1988 graphic novel in which the Joker says that if he must have a past, he "[prefers] it to be multiple choice." He makes "a direct allusion to this dialogue in suggesting that—as many fans have speculated—Arthur Fleck might not necessarily be who we think he is."[28] Sound familiar?

The noun, "paradise," in Benjamin's reading of unredeemed history, connotes an Edenic image of the past that is not out of sync with "angels"—a redemptive moment that rescues what is lost—a world without suffering. There is no question that there is a theologically inspired side to Benjamin and the allegorical-figurative nature of redemption is part of his thinking about liberation from the continuous denial of material oppression. But there is suffering in *Modern Times*, and any notion of "paradise" is in it is imageless; rather, Benjamin's notion of "paradise," however, is in alignment with Chaplin's comoedic *imago mundi* in its etymological meaning as "park"—"an *enclosed* tract of land"[29] (emphasis added). "All I need to make a comedy," Chaplin asserts, a film—a world, "is a park, a policeman and a pretty girl" (*My Autobiography* 159).

The storytelling Tramp is not all that far removed from the "story" he voices and mimes. He is both allegorical and figurative; his performance contains meaning that redeems what is being configured as lost.

Chaplin's voice which we hear for the first time rescues the forgetful Tramp whose voice it is as well—the gibberish—there is still a semblance of his character in this absurd sounding nonsense that parallels his dramatically overdone gestures and expressions. But the spectator also has the choice of "hearing" the Tramp's gibberish as art. From this aesthetic standpoint, then, Benjamin's reading of modern history and the contemporary present shows that the "content" of a work of art goes beyond the "form" and carries the "form" along with it into the present; the past is littered below the angel whose wings cannot be closed to the suffering below.

The otherness that Chaplin "gets inside" at the end, and in the end, allows us to perceive an otherness: the *imago mundi* of the café shows that

> the world we live in is cluttered with debris, all attempts at synthesis notwithstanding. There are no wholes in this world; rather it consists of bits of chance events whose flow substitutes for meaningful continuity. Correspondingly, individual consciousness must be thought of as an aggregate of splinters of beliefs and sundry activities; and since the life of the mind lacks structure, impulses from psychosomatic regions are apt to surge up and fill the interstices. Fragmented individuals *act out their parts* in fragmentized reality.
>
> (Kracauer 298)

Thus, the Tramp improvises. His gibberish, "an aggregate of splinters" that includes fragments of Italian, French and Spanish (sounding) words, is repeated in his gestures that "surge up and fill the interstices"; even in this monumental and transformative moment, a mime is still a mime; its essence, articulate movement.

Klee's angel, according to Benjamin, "is about to move away from something he is fixedly contemplating." The crucial phrase in Benjamin's description is "about to move." The three words can conjure for our reading of the Tramp's dumbfounding final act; and in the sequence wherein he is redefined, they are a poignant observation of his language and its nuanced movement. He toys with us—plays with us—suspends the movement; and then, unexpectedly, he is about to speak for the first time.

Klee's angel was made in 1920. In *My Trip Abroad* (1922), Chaplin asserts: the "only way I notice things is on the run. Whatever keenness of perception I have is momentary, fleeting. I observe all in ten minutes or not at all" (101). There is a similarity between the angel's "wondrous" eyes and the Tramp's "Kino" eye since he is performing for a camera—and once again he is more than aware of being watched—and he is more than aware of the fact that for a moment he is a spectacle. Klee's angel, however, is, aloof, innocent of complicity. The Tramp, on the other hand, is an accomplice to history—to his past in *Modern Times*—and so is the enigmatic Arthur Fleck in the beginning; as "Joker" he becomes, like Klee's angel, directly expressive of his moment in time. Moreover, Klee's "angel"—and the way the figure is composed (about to move)—is also a kind of "entertainer" in the sense that when we look at the image, the spectator-viewer formulates the expectation that something is about to happen. From this vantage point, the hesitating Tramp constructs our expectations towards his imminent performance spectacle.[30] And with the gamine, he perhaps finds his place.

We will recall that Siegfried Kracauer explains the happy endings of Chaplin's films as injunctions that say "we must go on living." For a comedian who sees the world as it is this is all one can say. And the Tramp now stands out as an example—like he always did—not of innocence but of what to avoid. *Modern Times* illuminates its age in so far as it reveals the "innocent" Tramp for who he actually is, rather than for who he seems. His final performance hits us almost like an editorial—it is that clear and obvious. "A pretty girl and a gay old man."

Chaplin causes a similar fracture in *The Great Dictator*, again at the end of the film, when he speaks "as Chaplin" and delivers a "plea for decency and brotherhood": "More than machinery, we need humanity! More than cleverness, we need kindness and gentleness!" Such a plea would not be out of place in *Modern Times*. Chaplin's "coda" is itself an injunction that galvanizes the dialectical apposition of the two films. Still, it "is fatal," Roger Ebert contends, "when Chaplin drops his comic persona, abruptly changes the tone of the film, and leaves us wondering how long he is going to talk (a question that should never arise during a comedy). The movie plays like a comedy followed by an editorial.

Chaplin," according to Ebert, "nevertheless was determined to keep the speech; it might have been his reason for making the film." "To me," Chaplin points out, "the funniest thing in the world is to ridicule impostors."[31] Clearly, in *Modern Times*, the joke's on *the director*.

The way is ready-made for the two main characters as they run for their escape—there is now a clear path from the dressing room to the exit—the patrons stand on the one side, like cheering crowds at a football game. They are now accomplices who watch a tragedy that the Tramp quickly transforms into a comedy, knocking over chairs, blocking the path they are taking behind them and keeping the "authorities" who would "detain" them at bay. "In the creation of comedy," Chaplin writes, "it is paradoxical that tragedy stimulates the spirit of ridicule; because ridicule, I suppose, is an attitude of defiance: we must laugh in the face of our helplessness against the forces of nature—or go insane" (*My Autobiography* 299). This comedian who sees, shows us a new day, like all the rest: "Dawn."

The "happy ending" of *Modern Times* is also self-reflexive and introspective. The Tramp plays many roles built around his pursuit of the gamine—"a girl" as observed and defined by morality, law and the authorities—in fact, he resuscitates his "tramp" persona when it suits him—it is a role he transforms into a factory worker—that is how we first see him—goofing around and imitating Pan gone berserk; a shipyard worker who botches the job; a mechanic's assistant who unleashes machine-like violence on his colleague; a night watchman "on a date."[32] As the plot advances, so does his nefarious past. It seems the gamine, "Ellen Peterson," has just cause to ponder her place in the end. Dejected, she wonders: "What's the use of trying?" as she bundles up their things for him. That is a loaded question—it is not rhetorical; it is a sudden realization that she too has played a role in, and succumbed to, the Tramp's scheming and that she is about to continue to play another for him in her new dress and "identity." "Buck up—never say die. We'll get along!" is the Tramp's indifferent and cold response, which he delivers, of course, not as a speaking character, but as a mime. Hardly a happy ending.

The Tramp's final smile, contrary to that of the Joker, is only a half-smile, and not a genuine one at that—the audience sees him hesitating, before he "puts it on." He remains merely "A tramp, a gentleman, a poet, a dreamer, a lonely fellow, always hopeful of romance and adventure" (*My Autobiography* 146). At the very least, his and Ellen's future is open. This is in fact the most anarchic image in the film, and if they are anarchists, as some critics have said, then here is where that anarchy is birthed: on the open road before an unknown horizon. Their relationship may bear fruit, but that remains to be seen. And this closing image is far from the image and idea of the comfort of confinement the Tramp has so far aggressively sought. In the end, Chaplin finally got his "moral" and "beautiful" ending—with candour.

In this redemptive moment, the Tramp finally escapes the confines of being an "object" and is liberated in the end—with "Ellen." "You'll learn from her what your life's course will be" (Dante, "Canto 10") (Figure 3.3 and Figure 3.4).

Figure 3.3 Closing image (Tramp and Ellen on the divided highway) frontal

Figure 3.4 Image of Tramp and Ellen from behind

Chaplin said he did not want to make a revolution, only more films. In *Modern Times*, he manages to leave the revolution-making part with us, his audiences, ensuring that he can go on making films: the Tramp will be reborn as a Fascist dictator in his next film. And he will keep on making his films, and we will go to see them.

Notes

1 "I saw little virtue in a system in which man must work to live" (*My Autobiography* 271).
2 See www.etymonline.com/word/gibberish
3 From this standpoint, even Picasso's *Guernica* is comoedic.
4 "A Humble Remonstrance (1884)," 217.
5 David Robinson commentary.
6 See *My Autobiography* 196–198.
7 Eliot in "Tradition and the Individual Talent."
8 "A basic principle of modern state capitalism is that the costs and risks are socialized to the extent possible, while profit is privatized" (Noam Chomsky). https://ideapod.com/noam-chomsky-quotes/
9 *Joker*, too, is an origin story.
10 *Joker* uses the grittier Jimmy Durante version (1965) immediately after Arthur Fleck's first performance as a stand-up comedian.
11 David Robinson in "Filming Modern Times." www.charliechaplin.com/en/articles/6-Filming-Modern-Times. Accessed 4 Feb. 2021. The text for the scene

is housed in the Chaplin archives and is read word-for-read on the commentary track of the Criterion edition of *Modern Times*. In the original ending, the gamine's longing for the Tramp is conveyed by imagining herself chasing after him; this compares with Arthur Fleck's psychosis—his imaginary girlfriend.

12 An important part of this social authority includes the

> voices in the movie [that] are channeled through other media. The ruthless steel tycoon talks over closed-circuit television, a crackpot inventor brings in a recorded sales pitch, and so on. The only synced sound is Charlie's famous tryout as a singing waiter.
>
> (Ebert)

The trajectory is disastrous in Modern Times; it is the nihilist trajectory in *Joker*. "One puts on vocally the technology of the age, much as Chaplin did in his way, as if in revenge and reversal" (McLuhan 118).

13 David Robinson in "Filming *Modern Times*."
14 Jerry Zaslove (personal correspondence). Zaslove's pithy expression refers to and summarizes Maurice Merleau-Ponty's discussion in his essay, "Cézanne's Doubt," in which he asserts that "We can only see before us, and in the form of goals, what it is that we are—so that our life always has the form of a project or choice, and thus seems to us self-caused" (see https://faculty.uml.edu/rinnis/cezannedoubt.pdf).
15 Maurice Merleau-Ponty, "Cézanne's Doubt." http://txt-bk.info/wp-content/uploads/2018/11/cezannedoubt.pdf
16 It is inexplicable, and an injustice, that the actor who plays the part is not acknowledged in the credits.
17 Short for Konstantinos Gavras.
18 Nicholas Barber. "The Great Dictator: The Film That Dared to Laugh at Hitler." *BBC.com/Culture*, 5 Feb. 2021. www.bbc.com/culture/article/20210204-the-great-dictator-the-film-that-dared-to-laugh-at-hitler. Accessed 9 Feb. 2021.
19 The scene outside the police station is not without a comically grotesque aspect. We are able to see the Tramp's hands as he spins her around. They are lean, but they are also old. One can discern veins. This instance of "unstaged" reality furthers the staged reality of the plot we have been following. Chaplin was 47 years old in 1936; in *Modern Times*, his love interest, the "gamine" is, literally, "a naughty child."
20 "Is not the Tramp wholly a David figure?" (Kracauer 281).
21 Unlike Fleck when he is introduced by Murray Franklin (Robert de Niro) at the end—he knows why he is there.
22 "I turned to Beatrice at my right, / to see in her some gesture, word or sign, / to show me what my duty now must be, / and saw the light within her eye so clear, / so full of laughter that her look and air / defeated all that these, before, had been" (Dante, "Canto 18").
23 www.etymonline.com/word/gibberish
24 See William Butler Yates. "The Second Coming." www.poetryfoundation.org/poems/43290/the-second-coming
25 Actress and writer Phoebe Waller-Bridge praised *Joker*, stating,

> I think the reason people got so uncomfortable is because it feels too true, too raw. I was watching it and thinking to myself, God, if this came out a year into Obama's time in office, I don't think we'd be feeling as worried about it.

"Buck up—never say die. We'll get along." That was the Tramp "then." The obvious and "present" truth underlying the film *Joker* is that perhaps we have taken the Tramp's lesson for granted. *Meanwhile.*

26 www.studiobinder.com/blog/joker-script-screenplay-pdf-download/
27 www.studiobinder.com/blog/joker-script-screenplay
28 See "Joker Director Finally Explains That Crucial Last Scene." www.looper.com/169166/joker-director-finally-explains-that-last-crucial-scene/
29 Like the space in a frame.

> Let's say there is always something outside the frame, lurking or knocking or waiting, unwelcome perhaps or unnoticed—the stranger or the strangeness that refuses to come inside, or that we ignore, or deliberately keep at bay. What happens if the frame breaks and this thing, this otherness, gets inside? Doesn't everything change, the frame as well as each thing it once held apart?
>
> (Ann Lauterbach)

30 In Jerry Zaslove's view, the Tramp plays a role that an anarchist might play, who "plays innocent and dismantles the place, or it dismantles." The problem with this view is that it implies that the Tramp has both agency and autonomy when, in fact, he denies both. Zaslove has in mind here the Formalist technique of defamiliarization or making strange. "The essence of Chaplin," he argues, "is a sensual strange-making—from his mechanized walk to his contradictory wardrobe. He is also fond of using the wrong object for wrong purposes. Every gag is a lesson in making strange." The couple who own their home seem "normal." Inside "their" home, however, the Tramp breaks every rule of decorum—half-eating a piece of fruit that he has picked from a tree outside his open window, disposing of it by kicking it outside again after he's taken a bite, wiping his dirty hands on the interior curtains, summoning a cow and not knowing how to properly milk it (personal correspondence with Jerry Zaslove).
31 Cited in *"The Great Dictator*: The film that dared to laugh at Hitler" and attributed to *My Autobiography*.
32 That is how *Joker* describes their relationship in the script.

Postscript
Meanwhile

Modern Times is indeed more than the sum of its parts: its overarching narrative is the dehumanization of the individual which begins *in* "modern times"—the effect of industrialization and standardization on the human condition—the work of life in the age of mechanical reproducibility. We have emphasized that the Tramp's metamorphosis from a "factory worker" to a "singing waiter" is a result of his fortuitous encounter and relationship with the "gamine." *Modern Times* is a dark film; yet, we are meant to read its closing image of the "two tramps" in a hopeful light—as the continuation of the film's announced intent to produce "A story of industry, of individual enterprise—humanity crusading in the pursuit of happiness." The ending and closing images of *Modern Times*, however, divert from that narrative intent. We have come to care for Ellen because the Tramp merely appears to care about her, but the audience knows differently. In the end, that is really all that matters. Social utopian ideals and projects aside—"individual enterprise, humanity crusading in the pursuit of happiness"—all that is secondary now to what these two individuals have experienced—*together*; and, moreover, what they will continue experiencing and living toward—*together* in the future in times beyond the "modern." Happy endings are a convention of comoedic art. This one is also sobering. Meanwhile.

Here, we might recall Siegfried Kracauer's insight on the "happy endings" of Chaplin's films "as injunctions that say we must go on living." What is unique about the ending of *Modern Times* is its closing image of the Tramp and Ellen together: "Buck up—never say die. We'll get along!"—together but separate: they are walking along a divided highway, each on either side of the centre line.

Their future together is wide open—we are left wondering what comes next for them—even in the face of approaching storms. And Chaplin's closing image of the two of them is a far cry away from the film's opening images of factories, subways and sheep herding.

DOI: 10.4324/9780429323317-4

If Chaplin's *Modern Times* is dark, then Todd Phillips's post-modern film, *Joker*, is petrifying. The gamine rescues the Tramp—and by doing so, symbolically rescues humanity in the end, despite her despair. Arthur Fleck rescues no one; humanity—if it still exists for him—is merely a spectacle; a cruel joke at his expense. It is this point of view that separates the two films and renders the one, *Modern Times*, "comoedic" and the other, *Joker*, "tragic." We see the presentation of life as it is lived in Chaplin's film through the main characters' interactions with the abruptly changing situations into which they are thrown; in the latter film, we see a spectacle through the subjective eyes of an unreliable Arthur Fleck. Put another way, we know what we are laughing at when we see *Modern Times*. What are we laughing at when we see *Joker*? That question is more than rhetorical. *Joker* moves from the profound of the comoedic to the bitter and cynical grotesque that comic strip "Action Heroes" were invented to redeem.[1] Thomas Wayne, a wealthy industrialist running for mayor of Gotham City, supported by his elite friends present at the gala benefit in his theatre (the post-modern 21st century's famous 1%), says of Arthur Fleck and his supporters in the protesting mob in the city streets outside:

> Someone who is envious of those more fortunate than themselves. Yet they're too scared to show their own face. And until *those kind of people* change for the better, those of us who have made something of our lives will always look at those who haven't as nothing but clowns.
> (emphasis added)

The tragedy of the film is Fleck's loss of innocence. In the confusion and uncertainty of his time and his own place in it, a time in which society has reverted to a two-class system of "haves" and "have-nots," he has been made perfectly well aware that "A story of industry, of individual enterprise—humanity crusading in the pursuit of happiness" has become an outdated fantasy, whereas "What's the use of trying?" has become the motto of his day—despair has triumphed in a world that Frances Fukuyama described in his essay for the RAND Corporation in 1989 (which he would go on to embellish and publish as a book) called, *The End of History and the Last Man*.

Fleck's perception of Chaplin in the theatre is allegorical—it opens new ways of reading both works, especially Chaplin's. We learn that a relationship between one film and another is the cinema's most natural language—it is a language that learns to see the more one searches for it—a form of listening with the eyes. But films do more than reference and record—they also "remember"; and the final work illuminates not only what is remembered but also the construction of that memory. The reason *Joker* is devastating to us is because the film destroys history, as indeed all comic book characters do. They are imaginary characters in an imaginary world—complicit with a fantasy that negates history. Its main character, Arthur Fleck ("Joker"), is presented with two versions of his past: his mother's allegation that he is the illegitimate son of an illicit affair she had with the scion of a wealthy industrialist's family (Thomas Wayne) and the official documents he wrests from a clerk at the civic records office, which "certify" that he was adopted by his mother and abused and neglected as a child. Were those documents created at the behest of the Wayne family to falsify history and sanitize their reputation, or are they "authentic?" Neither Arthur Fleck nor we the audience know, so we watch how this uncertainty about his past destroys him as a character, appearing literally as his own double, twice, in *Joker's* very last scene at the mental hospital for the criminally insane where he has been confined. But Chaplin's character builds on his history—in his moment of elision, the "Little Tramp" will speak! Voice begets voice. And when the Tramp finally sings, he invites response. His voice changes our relationship with him. As a shot, it is Chaplin's least "trickiest"—it is merely the Tramp performing in front of a camera—and yet, it affects us because the Tramp's past, and Chaplin's, has lead him here. Thus, *Modern Times* introduces the Tramp to sound; introduces Chaplin to sound. In one last nod to Chaplin, Phillips ends his film in a flood of white space and light, fading into a void of nothingness, the visual equivalent to silence. And in Fleck's closing scene, we see him "divided."

In comparing the two films as we have done, two other works can come to mind that show how quoting and adapting a classic film like *Modern Times* in a modern version begets art and enters into life. The first is the 2009 film, *Night of the Living Dead: Reanimated*; the second, Werner Herzog's 1979 film *Nosferatu*. These two films—and there are others—are remakes of originals: the first, a remake of George A. Romero's 1968 film, *Night of the Living Dead*; and Herzog's, a remake of F.W. Murnau's 1922 film *Nosferatu*.[2] What does one see when one looks back at the past from the vantage point of the present through the films which make that happen? The answer, of course, is the "contemporary," which begets another question: what is the contemporary?

In the first example, *Night of the Living Dead: Reanimated*, the film "features the work of various artists, animators, and filmmakers from around the globe" to recreate each scene in the original *Night of the Living Dead*. The remade ("reanimated") film follows the original script and its score. Each animator recreates individual scenes in their own style. Once assembled, the film becomes disorienting because it is the same and not the same film simultaneously. It is an exercise in writing the script after the fact of the film. One learns to see the present in "retrospect." One discovers and sees a new world through retrospective images in the interstices where all films reside. In the meanwhile.

Herzog's remake of the Murnau classic vampire film is compelling on these grounds, especially since the latter film is not a silent film, although cinematically, it experiences itself as one. Herzog's version in its dissimilarity is so close to the original work; it's uncanny. But the differences and similarities are always in the nuances. These two films show that a close—unsentimental—reading of previous art constructs and enacts both a way of seeing life as it was lived in its own time and as it is experienced in the present of its making.

In Chaplin's comedy *Modern Times*, one more easily identifies with the episodes and less with the characters. This is why Chaplin's Tramp character stands out: not because he is funny but because of the tension that exists between the character and the situation—what Chaplin calls "candour":

> What appears to be sane is really insane, and if you can make that poignant enough they love it. The audience recognises it as a farce on life, and they laugh at it in order not to die from it, in order not to weep. *It's a question of that mysterious thing called candour coming in.* An old man slips on a banana and falls slowly and stumbles and we don't laugh. But if it's done with a pompous well-to-do gentleman who has exaggerated pride, then we laugh. All embarrassing situations are funny, especially if they're treated with humour. With clowns you can expect anything outrageous to happen. But if a man goes into a restaurant, and he thinks he's very smart but he's got a big hole in his pants—if that is treated humorously, it's bound to be funny. Especially if it's done with dignity and pride.
>
> (Meryman 362; emphasis added)

"Candour" is the opposite of spectacle. And since *Modern Times* is not a tragedy, we do not need to worry about "identifying" with this "gentle little fellow." This, too, is what John Berger means when he asserts that "every image embodies a way of *seeing*" (10; emphasis added). He is saying that the "meaning" of a work—an image—cannot be understood without both the autonomy of art and the critical spirit of the author and artist. *Joker* is thoroughly saturated in and by the view that the epoch of modernism brings us into the post-modern when the fate and destiny of both art and the individual are at one and the same time struggling in new historical conditions not always of the individual or his/her society's own making. Arthur Fleck's anxieties were born in "modern times." This is why it makes sense to revisit *Modern Times* from the vantage point of the current post-modern *Joker*.

Chaplin laughed at Riefenstahl's film in real time—in real life; Arthur Fleck—at the very moment of his metamorphosis from an innocent loser to a psychopathic killer—is laughing in a film, at a film.

Where modern time *in "Modern Times"* is imagined as possibly utopic, post-modern time—our time after *Modern Times*—Arthur Fleck's time—has become dystopic. *Modern times* to us now might as well be ancient history. What happened?

That question has been answered by our close reading of scenes that reveal shifts of perception and attention, helping to discern the film's structure from within. In fact, a poignant aesthetic question that should be asked after any film experience is—*what happened*? The question is not naïve but assumes there was something that remains of the experience.

If the comoedic is the presentation of life as it is lived, then a literal reading of life as it is presented in *Modern Times* illuminates the "candour" of work *and* life in the age of mechanical reproducibility. All the challenges involved in writing about any one of Chaplin's films, especially *Modern Times*, become painfully obvious—that Chaplin is a conventional filmmaker. He asserts that he wants to do his own thinking, to have the freedom to think for himself. That is, Chaplin, the "director," and his insight illuminates his "wincingly naïve" Tramp character (Ross 20). Chaplin, "the Tramp," wants to be looked at and looked after—he is comfortable with confinement—a world view that is challenged by the presence of the gamine and a world view that is rejected in the film's closing image.

In a subtle gesture, Chaplin sets up his ending in the first title card that names the Tramp in *Modern Times* as a "factory worker." He gives him a place in social reality as a worker in a factory in "modern times." He goes "crazy" and convalesces but returns to his "cinematic" identity as the Tramp; and he remains a Tramp up until his final act.

In *Modern Times*, Chaplin's character can also be interpreted through reference to Walter Benjamin's notion of fate and character; fate relates to "misfortune (rather than to happiness, which would be a way of escaping fate) and belongs therefore to the world of the law"—the law pursues the gamine and the Tramp both inadvertently and advertently engages the authority of the law in the Tramp's eagerness to return to a home he feels comfortable with, while both "pursue happiness" (*Reflections* xxvi). The Tramp will become a new character at the expense of his fate, thanks in large part to the gamine. But Benjamin's point in his characterization of fate is related to technology as a fated aspect of modern times: we cannot escape from it. Fleck as Fleck is crushed by socio-economic pressures; as Joker, he masters them. The Tramp and gamine endure, but their endurance is contingent—uncertain. Their fate transcends fate. They are left standing—"Bucking up"—in the face of fate.

If we consider *Modern Times* comoedically, we discern a story that is less a comedy and more a fictionalized documentary of "these modern times" because it shows them as experienced and lived. Both the Tramp and gamine learn to see life anew in *Modern Times*. That is what they have in the end—their pursuit. "Work" continues to elude them.

Seeing is learning how to see. This study of *Modern Times* shows that "learning to see Chaplin" is learning, in part, to see film. Chaplin wants his films to be "seen" as the art of seeing. Through shifts in perception and reversals, one perceives and sees difference in films and sees differently after we understand that we have undergone an experience. Images and scenes in a film projected onto the screen's surface are a history made of other scenes and images. Image begets image; films beget films—they often see more than their spectators think they see—the image that is seen is also the image that is unseen. A literal and unsentimental reading of Chaplin's ending of *Modern Times* takes up this act of seeing in order to show what remains to be seen or what has not been seen before. As Charlie Chaplin's contemporary, Gertrude Stein, put it: "Let me recite what history teaches. History teaches." And as Chaplin reminds us, "There are more valid facts and details in works of art" that reveal the struggle to become a person (*My Autobiography* 320).

Notes

1 It is no accident that the very first comic-strip "*Action*" or "*Super-hero*"—*The Phantom*, was created in 1936—the very year the final cut of *Modern Times* was released for screening.
2 "Brunchsquatch," the premiere episode in Season 8 of *Bob's Burgers*, is another recent example. It features animation inspired by submissions from the Bob's Burgers Fan Art AKA Fart contest.

Works cited

Abraham Lincoln in the Post-Heroic Era: History and Memory in Late Twentieth-Century America. The University of Chicago Press Books, press.uchicago.edu/ucp/books/book/chicago/A/bo5820691.html.
Ackroyd, Peter. *Charlie Chaplin.* Chatto & Windus, 2014.
Acuna, Kristen. "12 Details and References You May Have Missed in *Joker.*" *Insider.com,* 3 Oct. 2019, www.insider.com/joker-dc-references-easter-eggs-breakdown-2019-10. Accessed 31 May 2021.
Adorno, Theodor W. "Chaplin Times Two." *The Essential Chaplin: Perspectives in the Life and Art of the Great Comedian,* edited by Richard Schickel. Ivan R. Dee, 2006, pp. 267–272.
Adorno, Theodor W., and Max Horkheimer. *Towards a New Manifesto.* Verso, 2019.
Aristotle. *Poetics,* translated by Malcolm Heath. Penguin Books, 1996.
Austerlitz, Saul. "Modern Times: Exit the Tramp." *The Current,* The Criterion Collection, 10 Nov. 2010, www.criterion.com/current/posts. Accessed 11 Jan. 2021.
Barber, Nicholas. "The Great Dictator: The Film That Dared to Laugh at Hitler." *BBC.com/Culture, BBC,* 5 Feb. 2021, www.bbc.com/culture/article/20210204-the-great-dictator-the-film-that-dared-to-laugh-at-hitler. Accessed 9 Feb. 2021.
Benjamin, Walter. "On the Concept of History." *Selected Writings Volume IV: 1938–1940,* edited and translated by Howard Eiland and Michael D. Jennings. Harvard University Press, 2003, pp. 389–400, https://warwick.ac.uk/fac/arts/english/currentstudents/undergraduate/modules/fulllist/second/en229/benjamin_on_the_concept_of_history.pdf.
———. *One-Way Street,* edited by Michael W. Jennings and translated by Edmund Jephcott. Harvard University Press, 2016.
———. *Reflections: Essays, Aphorisms, Autobiographical Writings,* edited by Peter Demetz. Mariner Books, Houghton Mifflin Harcourt, 2019.
———. "The Work of Art in the Age of Mechanical Reproduction." *Illuminations: Essays and Reflections,* edited by Hannah Arendt. Mariner Books, Houghton Mifflin Harcourt, 2019, pp. 166–195.
Berger, John. *Ways of Seeing.* Penguin Books, 1972.
Bourne, Mark. "The Chaplin Collection." *The DVD Journal | DVD News, Reviews, Rumors, and Commentary,* www.dvdjournal.com/reviews/m/moderntimes.shtml. Accessed 16 Jan. 2021.

Works cited

Brooks, Atkinson. "Charlie Chaplin." *The Essential Chaplin: Perspectives in the Life and Art of the Great Comedian*, edited by Richard Schickel. Ivan R. Dee, 2006, pp. 219–222.
Bürger, Peter. *Theory of the Avant-Garde*, translated by Michael Shaw. University of Minnesota Press, 1994.
Caro-Morente, Jaime. "The Political Culture of the IWW during Its First 20 Years." *Industrial Worker*, vol. 114, no. 1780/3, 2017, www.academia.edu/37816171/The_political_culture_of_the_IWW_during_its_first_20_years. Accessed 24 May 2021.
Chaplin, Charlie. *A Comedian Sees the World*, edited by Lisa Stein Haven. University of Missouri Press, 2014.
———. *Interviews*, edited by Kevin J. Hayes. University Press of Mississippi, 2005.
———. *My Trip Abroad*. Harper and Brothers, 1922.
———. *My Wonderful Visit*. E-book. Hurst & Blackett, Ltd., 2013.
"Commentary track (David Robinson)." *Modern Times*. The Criterion Collection, New York, 2010.
Critchley, Simon. *Tragedy, the Greeks, and Us*. Vintage, 2020.
Dante, Alighieri. *The Divine Comedy*, translated and edited by Robin Kirkpatrick. Penguin, 2013.
Demers, Jason. *Collecting Intensities: The Arrival of French Theory in America, 1970s*. York University, PhD dissertation, 2009, https://central.bac-lac.gc.ca/.item?id=NR64888&op=pdf&app=Library&oclc_number=780359059. Accessed 17 June 2021.
Duchamp, Marcel. "The Creative Act." *Marcel Duchamp: Salt Seller: The Writings of Marcel Duchamp*, edited by Michel Sanouillet and Elmer Peterson. Thames and Hudson, 1975, pp. 138–140.
Ebert, Roger. "The Great Dictator Movie Review (1940)." *The Great Dictator Movie Review (1940)*. *rogerebert.com*, 27 Sept. 1972, www.rogerebert.com/reviews/great-movie-the-great-dictator-1940. Accessed 17 Feb. 2021.
———. "Modern Times Movie Review & Film Summary (1972)." *Movie Review & Film Summary (1972)*. *rogerebert.com*, 25 Jan. 1972, www.rogerebert.com/reviews/modern-times-1972. Accessed 29 Jan. 2021.
Eisenstein, Sergei. "Montage and Architecture." Translated by Michael Glenny. *Assemblage*, vol. 10, Dec. 1989, pp. 110–131, https://doubleoperative.files.wordpress.com/2009/12/eisenstein-sergei-m-_montage-and-architecture.pdf. Accessed 22 Feb. 2021.
Elsaesser, Thomas. "Siegfried Kracauer's Affinities." *Necsus-ejms.org*, Spring 14_#Traces, 16 May 2014, https://necsus-ejms.org/siegfried-kracauers-affinities/. Accessed 29 Jan. 2021.
Ferguson, Otis. "Hallelujah, Bum Again." *The Essential Chaplin: Perspectives in the Life and Art of the Great Comedian*, edited by Richard Schickel. Ivan R. Dee, 2006, pp. 228–231.
Foltz, Jonathan. "In Search of Lost Plots: On Viktor Shklovsky." *Los Angeles Review of Books*, 24 Oct. 2012, https://lareviewofbooks.org/article/in-search-of-lost-plots-on-viktor-shklovsky/. Accessed 28 Jan. 2020.
Fox, Audrey. "What Child Is This: The Enduring Legacy of Charlie Chaplin's The Kid." *rogerebert.com*, 8 Jan. 2021, www.rogerebert.com/features/what-

child-is-this-the-enduring-legacy-of-charlie-chaplins-the-kid. Accessed 29 Jan. 2021.

Frenkel, Vera. "Benign Ignorance." *Artscanada*, vol. 34, nos. 214/215, May–June 1977, pp. 27–30.

Greene, Graham. "Modern Times." *The Essential Chaplin: Perspectives in the Life and Art of the Great Comedian*, edited by Richard Schickel. Ivan R. Dee, 2006, pp. 225–227.

Han, Byung-Chul. *The Disappearance of Rituals: A Topology of the Present*, translated by Daniel Steuer. Polity, 2020.

Hansen, Miriam Bratu. "Introduction." *Theory of Film: The Redemption of Physical Reality*. Princeton University Press, 1996, pp. vii–xlv.

Hoberman, J. "After the Gold Rush: Chaplin at 100." *The Essential Chaplin: Perspectives in the Life and Art of the Great Comedian*, edited by Richard Schickel. Ivan R. Dee, 2006, pp. 297–304.

Hutchinson, Pamela. "*The Circus:* The Tramp in the Mirror." *The Current*, The Criterion Collection, 27 Sept. 2019, www.criterion.com/current/posts/6607-the-circus-the-tramp-in-the-mirror. Accessed 24 May 2021.

Joker, directed by Todd Phillips, performances by Joaquin Phoenix and Robert De Niro, Warner Bros, 2019.

"Joker Director Breaks Down the Opening Scene | Vanity Fair." *YouTube*, uploaded by Vanity Fair, 7 Oct. 2021, www.youtube.com/watch?v=awoQuVq2yYc.

Kirkpatrick, Robin. "Introduction." *The Divine Comedy*. Penguin, 2013, pp. ix–liv.

Kracauer, Siegfried. *Theory of Film: The Redemption of Physical Reality*. Oxford University Press, 1960.

Lauterbach, Ann. "The Night Sky II: A Column." *The American Poetry Review*, vol. 25, no. 6, 1996, pp. 9–16. *JSTOR*, www.jstor.org/stable/27782266. Accessed 29 Jan. 2021.

Lawrence, Bergreen. "Chaplin's Times." *The Harvard Crimson*, 24 Jan. 1972, www.thecrimson.com/article/1972/1/24/chaplins-times-pbablthough-charlie-chaplin-has/. Accessed 29 Jan. 2021.

Leyda, Jay. *Films Beget Films: A Study of the Compilation Film*. Hill and Wang, 1971.

Maland, Charles J. *Chaplin and American Culture: The Evolution of a Star Image*. Princeton University Press, 1989.

Manchel, Frank. *Film Study: An Analytical Bibliography* (Vol. 2). Associated University Press, 1990, pp. 1428–1429.

McLuhan, Marshall, and Wilfred Watson. *From Cliché to Archetype*, edited by W. Terrence Gordon. Gingko Press, Inc., 2011.

Merleau-Ponty, Maurice. "Cézanne's Doubt," http://txt-bk.info/wp-content/uploads/2018/11/cezannedoubt.pdf. Accessed 17 June 2021.

Meryman, Richard. "Chaplin Interviewed by Richard Meryman 1966." *Chaplin: Genius of the Cinema*. Harry N. Abrams, 2003, pp. 360–367.

Modern Times, directed by Charlie Chaplin, performances by Charlie Chaplin and Paulette Goddard, Charlie Chaplin Productions, 1936.

Morrison, Toni. "The Bird Is in Your Hands." *Nobelprize.org*, Nobel Media AB, 2013, www.nobelprize.org/prizes/literature/1993/morrison/lecture/. Accessed 23 June 2021.

Nabokov, Vladimir. *Think, Write, Speak: Uncollected Essays, Reviews, Interviews, and Letters*, edited by Brian Boyd and translated by Anastasia Tolstoy. Vintage International, 2019.

Robinson, David. *Chaplin: His Life and Art*. Collins, 1985.

———. "Filming Modern Times." *Charlie Chaplin Official Website*, www.charliechaplin.com/en/articles/6-Filming-Modern-Times. Accesses 5 June 2021.

Ross, Alex. "Wagner in Hollywood: A Composer's Fractured Legacy in Film." *The New Yorker*, 31 Aug. 2020, pp. 18–24.

Schickel, Richard. "Introduction: The Tramp Transformed." *The Essential Chaplin: Perspectives on the Life and Art of the Great Comedian*, edited by Richard Schickel.I.R. Dee, 2006, pp. 3–41.

Seifert, Jaroslav. "On the Pathetic and Lyrical State of Mind." *NobelPrize.org*, Nobel Media AB, 2020, www.nobelprize.org/prizes/literature/1984/seifert/lecture/. Accessed 19 Dec. 2020.

Shklovsky, Viktor. *Knight's Move*, translated by Richard Sheldon. Dalkey Archive Press, 2005.

———. *Literature and Cinematography*. Dalkey Archive Press, 2008.

———. *Third Factory*. Dalkey Archive Press, 2002.

———. *Viktor Shklovsky: A Reader*, edited by Alexandra Berlina. Bloomsbury, 2016.

Silberman, Marc. "Bertolt Brecht, Politics, and Comedy." *Social Research*, vol. 79, no. 1, 2012, pp. 169–188. *JSTOR*, www.jstor.org/stable/23350303. Accessed 23 May 2021.

Stevenson, Robert Louis. "A Humble Remonstrance." *Victorian Criticism of the Novel*, edited by Edwin M. Eigner and George J. Worth. Cambridge University Press, 1985, pp. 213–224.

Triumph of the Will, directed by Leni Riefenstahl, Reichsparteitag-Film, 1935.

Tyler, Parker. *Chaplin: Last of the Clowns*. Horizon Press, 1972.

Vance, Jeffrey. *Chaplin: Genius of the Cinema*. Harry N. Abrams, 2003.

Virilio, Paul. *Art and Fear*. Continuum, 2006.

Warshow, Robert. *The Immediate Experience: Movies, Comics, Theatre, and Other Aspects of Popular Culture*. Harvard University Press, 2001.

Weissman, Stephen. *Chaplin: A Life*. Arcade Publishing, 2008.

Zaslove, Jerry. "Counterfeit and the Use of Literature." *West Coast Review*, 1967, pp. 5–6.

Žižek, Slavoj. *The Relevance of the Communist Manifesto*. Polity, 2019.

———. *Trouble in Paradise: From the End of History to the End of Capitalism*. Penguin, 2014.

Index

Ackroyd, Peter 66
Adorno, Theodor W. 72
aesthetic experience [Zaslove] 99n30
Angelus Novus (Klee) 89–90, 92, 94
Aristotle 30, 86
Arkham State Hospital 26, 92
Arnheim, Rudolf 49
Austerlitz, Saul 73
authoritarianism xii, 2, 8, 68
automatons 81

Barber, Nicholas 85
"Beatrice" 89, 98n22
benign ignorance 12
Benjamin, Walter 1, 12, 89–90, 93, 94, 104
Berger, John x, 103
Bergson, Henri 39
Bezos, Jeff 72
Billows feeding machine 6–11, 63, 73
Billows, J. Widdecombe 73
Blake, William xiv
Brecht, Bertolt 91
Breton, André x
Brooks, Mel 85
bullfight 81–83
Buñuel, Luis xiii

"candour" xiv, 96, 103–104
Capitalist president-boss 63, 81
chance meetings 53
Chaplin, Charlie: camera set-up 15–16; direction 16–17; economic theory 68, 71–72, 92; exchange between Gertrude Stein and 14; film aesthetic xv, 14–17, 30–31, 34, 48–49, 68, 75–79, 82–83, 87–88, 94–96, 101–102, 105; mention of feeding machine 8–9; naïveté xii; passages from autobiography 14; political vision 14, 19–20; on poverty 1; recollection of bullfight 81–83; sentimental radicalism 20; on time-saving 15–16; travel memoirs 68; viewing Riefenstahl's *Triumph of the Will* xiii, 104; *see also* titles of individual works
character 104
Churchill, Winston 75
City Lights (Chaplin) 24
Comedian Sees the World, A (Chaplin) 68, 75, 80
"communist" 19–20, 22, 25, 27
"comoedic" xiv, 15, 27, 30, 37, 46, 54, 70–72, 75, 79–82, 85, 87, 100–101, 104
"conflict and collision" 13
criminal xi, 5, 35
Critchley, Simon 30–31

Daniderff, Léo 87
Dante Alighieri 15, 98n22
Dark Knight Rises, The (Nolan) 79–80
David 9, 87
defamiliarization 38, 71, 99n30
dehumanization xii, 19–20, 100
De Niro, Robert 51
Depression 9, 29, 36, 71
Detroit 5
Disney, Walt 47

Divine Comedy (Dante Alighieri) 15
doubleness 10–11, 31n4, 32n8
dream home 37, 42–44, 61

Ebert, Roger 95, 98n12
efficiency 3, 11
Einstein, Albert 75
Eisenstein, Sergei 13, 14
Elsaesser, Thomas 49
End of History and the Last Man, The (Fukuyama) 101
Essential Chaplin, The (Schickel) xi

fabulous coincidences 53
fascism xiii, 20, 68
fate 104
feeding machine 6–11, 64–66, 73
Fleck, Arthur xi–xii, xiii, xiv, xv–xvi, 2, 9, 11, 13, 18, 26, 38, 39, 48–53, 77, 78, 79, 82, 92–93, 94, 101, 102, 103–104
Fleck, Penny xi–xii
Ford, Henry 3
Fordism 92
Frankenstein (Shelley) xiv
Franklin, Murray 51
Frenkel, Vera 12
Fukuyama, Frances 101

gamin 1, 23–25, 28, 68
gamine xiv, xvi, 4, 5, 8–9, 17, 24–25, 28, 31, 34–37, 40–50, 53–63, 65–66, 70, 73–77, 79–90, 92, 94–96
Gates, Bill 72
gibberish 89, 93–94
Goddard, Paulette xv, 1, 5, 25, 53
Goetz, Bernhard xiii
Gold Rush, The (Chaplin) 24
Goliath 9, 87
Great Dictator, The (Chaplin) xiii, xvi, 6, 20, 68, 95
Griffith, D.W. 14, 48

Hamlet (Shakespeare) 49
Hansen, Miriam Bratu 69
happiness xii, xiii, 1, 5, 13, 104
"happy ending" 77, 79–80, 95–96
Hardy, Oliver 67
herded sheep 1–2, 16, 100
Herzog, Werner 102–103

Hitler, Adolph xiii
Hooverville 57
Horkheimer, Max 72
House Un-American Activities Committee (HUAC) 20

"idle" 63
ignorance 12
imago mundi 93–94
inauthentic 1
individual xii, 1, 6, 19, 32n8, 39, 41, 66, 72, 94, 100, 101, 103
industrialization x, xiii, 3–4, 11, 20, 64, 70, 100
Ingraham, Lloyd 73, 83–85

jerky movements 10, 38
Joker (Phillips) xi–xv, 1, 9–10, 11, 13, 17, 18, 26, 37, 38, 39, 48–53, 77, 78, 79, 82, 92–93, 94, 101, 102, 103–104

Keaton, Buster 67
Killing Joke, The (Moore) 93
Klee, Paul 89–90, 92, 94
"Kracauer's Affinities" (Elsaesser) 49
Kracauer, Siegfried 17, 48–49, 69, 87, 94, 95, 100

Laing, R.D. 11
Laurel, Stanley 67
Lauterbach, Ann 89, 99n29
Leyda, Jay xi
"liberal views" 19, 80
Lincoln, Abraham 29
Littlest Rebel, The (Butler) 29

machine age xiv, 12
machinery 6, 7, 9, 11–13, 19, 42, 58, 62–65, 70, 72–73, 81, 95
machines x, 6–13, 63–66
Maeterlinck, Maurice 75
making strange 99n30
Marx Brothers 47
McGlynn, Frank 29
McLuhan, Marshall 6
mechanic 62–66, 73, 95
mechanical reproduction 12
mechanic's assistant" 62–66, 73, 95
mechanization xiv, 4, 11–12, 90
Mickey Mouse 47, 54

Index

Miller, Lee 80
modernity xiii–xiv, 1, 3, 17–18
Modern Times (Chaplin): cafeteria scene 35, 74; Capitalist president-boss. 3–4, 6–7, 11; cocaine 26–27; "comedy" of xii, 69–79; critique of "modern times" xiv, 39, 69–71; critique of socialism 20; deconstruction x–xvi; dream home sequence 37, 42–44; ending 75–79, 88–96, 100; factory assembly line 3–4, 9–10; feeding machine 6–11, 64–66; flag 17–18, 19–23, 26, 31; gamin 1, 23–25, 28, 68; gamine xiv, xvi, 4, 5, 8–9, 17, 24–25, 28, 31, 34–37, 40–50, 53–63, 65–66, 70, 73–77, 79–90, 92, 94–96; historicity xi; jailbreak 27–28, 74; jail cafeteria scene 26–27; mechanical salesman 6–8; mechanic's assistant 62–66, 73, 95; mental breakdown 9–13; montage of modern life 15–19, 80–81; night watchman xi, xiv, 5, 46–53, 95; opening images 1–3, 100; pocket watch 62–63; prison 25–31; ramshackle home 57–62, 74; role of women 53–55, 60; roller skating sequence 47–53; "steam shovel operator" gag 74; "Trouble outside" scene 28; waiter 5; workers' protest 13, 19–23
moral beauty 75–78, 79
Motor City 5
Murnau, F.W. 102–103
Musk, Elon 72
My Autobiography (Chaplin) 87
My Trip Abroad (Chaplin) 68, 94

Nabokov, Vladimir 67
New Yorker (magazine) xiii
Night of the Living Dead (Romero) 102
Night of the Living Dead (Schneider) 102–103
night watchman xi, xiv, 5, 46–53, 95
Nolan, Christopher 79–80
Nosferatu (Herzog) 102–103
Nosferatu (Murnau) 102–103

Obama, Barack H. 98n25
"Occupy Movement" xiii, 73
Olivier, Laurence 49
Outline of History (Wells) 88

Pan 13, 83, 95
pantomimic 75, 89
"paradise" 93
Peterson, Ellen xvi, 77, 86, 87, 95–96, 100
Phillips, Todd xi–xii, 1, 2, 17, 18, 26, 49, 73, 78, 82, 92–93, 101, 102
pocket watch 62–63
poetics 30–31
Poetics (Aristotle) 86
"polite" 10, 32n8, 36–38, 44, 45, 56
post-modern times xi, xiv, xv, 2, 4, 10–11, 36, 39, 41, 49, 52, 69, 73, 77, 78, 79, 82, 90, 93, 101, 103–104
poverty 1
pre-modern times 1–2

ramshackle home 57–62, 74
restaurant sequence 63, 70, 73
Riefenstahl, Leni xiii, xv, 20, 68, 104
Robinson, David 1, 24, 53–54, 64, 74, 75
Romero, George A. 102
Ross, Alex xiii

Schickel, Richard xi, xv, 8, 20–22
Selina (Ann Hathaway) 79–80
Shakespeare, William 34, 49
Shelley, Mary xiv
shipyard worker xi, 5, 31, 95
Shklovsky, Viktor 1, 30, 78
Siegler, Karl 33n19
staged reality 48, 52
standardization xiv, 3, 4, 7, 11–12, 40, 42, 68, 90, 100
Stein, Gertrude 14, 17
Superman 87
Symons, Stéphane 38–39

Tarzan (comic strip) 3, 13
Temple, Shirley 29
Theory of Film (Kracauer) 48, 87
"The Second Coming, The" (Yeats) 92
thief 8, 23, 34–35, 40, 45
Think, Write, Speak (Nabokov) 67
time 1, 4
Titine ("Je cherche après Titine") 87
"tragedy" 37, 69–70, 81, 86, 95, 101, 103
"Tramp Transformed, The" (Schickel) xi
tricky effects 14, 15, 17
Triumph of the Will, The (Riefenstahl) xiii, 20, 68

Trumpism 92
Tyler, Parker 66

uncinematic 17, 48–49
unstaged reality 48, 52–53

Vance, Jeffrey 29, 57
violence 8, 10–11, 26, 63, 64, 66, 73, 79, 81, 83, 92, 95

Wagner, Richard xiii
waiter xi, xv, xvi, 4, 5, 69, 73, 74, 78, 83–84, 86–87, 100

Waller-Bridge, Phoebe 98–99n25
Wayne, Bruce 79–80
Wayne Theatre 49–52
Wayne, Thomas xi, xiv, 48, 49, 50, 51, 79, 101, 102
Weismann, Stephen 20
Wells, H.G. 87–88

Yeats, William Butler 92

Zaslove, Jerry 98n14, 99n30
Žižek, Slavoj 72–73, 80
Zuckerberg, Mark 72–73